Read, Sing, and Play Along!

Children's Lullaby Songs

School Specialty Publishing

Columbus, Ohio

Activities and Design © 2006 School Specialty Publishing, a member of the School Specialty Family.

Send all inquiries to:
School Specialty Publishing
8720 Orion Place
Columbus, Ohio 43240-2111

ISBN 0-7696-4316-7

1 2 3 4 5 6 7 8 9 10 WAF 10 09 08 07 06

Table of Contents

Sheet Music 213

Bedtime Stories Log 319

Activities

Directions: Draw  and color a picture of how you look from head to toe.

Note to Parents: Encourage your child to look in a full-length mirror.

Directions: Write your name in the box.

Note to Parents: Encourage your child to print his or her name using a capital letter for the first letter and lower case letters for the rest of his or her name. This will help your child transition to kindergarten.

Directions: Write  your birthday and age on the cake. Draw and color a picture of your birthday wish in the puff of smoke.

Write your birthday and age.

I am ☐ years old.

Note to Parents: Talk with your child about when he or she was born. Revisit photographs of past birthdays.

© 2006 School Specialty Publishing

Read, Sing, and Play Along! Lullaby Songs   7

Name_____

Directions: Color ✎ the numbers 1, 2, and 3. Then, write ✏ the number 1, 2, or 3 in each box to put the pictures in order from youngest to oldest.

My Telephone Number

Name_____

Directions: Parents: Write ✏️ the child's telephone number. Then have him or her point to and say each number.

[   ]

Directions: Child: Copy ✏️ your telephone number in the box.

[   ]

Directions: Cut ✂️ and glue 🧴 the numbers in order on the telephone. Practice dialing your phone number on this telephone.

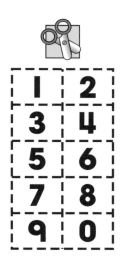

Note to Parents: Teach your child his or her phone number by setting it to a familiar song, such as *Twinkle, Twinkle Little Star*. Remember to teach the area code, too.

Left blank for cutting activity
on previous page.

Directions: Write  your address in the rectangle. Color the house the same color as the house or apartment where you live. Cut the bottom two pieces and glue their tabs to the tabs on the house. Open the doors and see what's inside!

Note to Parents: Before completing this page, take a walk around the block with your child. Point out your house number and the street sign with the name of your street.

Left blank for cutting activity
on previous page.

What Is Missing?

Directions: Find and circle  10 things in the top picture that are not in the bottom picture.

Note to Parents: Discuss all of the objects in the top picture. After completing the activity, if your child shows an interest, encourage him or her to list or draw the 10 items that are missing.

Directions: Draw ✏ a picture of your favorite place in your town. Add yourself in the picture doing what you like to do there.

Directions: Finish the following sentences.

My favorite place is [   ] .

I live in [, _____] .

city   state

Note to Parents: Talk with your child about places in your town. Revisit some of your favorites. Explore new places.

Color the House

Note to Parents: Read the following directions one at a time to your child. Allow time for your child to complete each task before reading the next direction.

Directions: Color the roof brown.

Color the chimney red.

Color the bushes green.

Draw a front door. Color it blue.

Draw 2 windows beside the door.

Draw yourself looking out a window.

Draw flowers in front of the house.

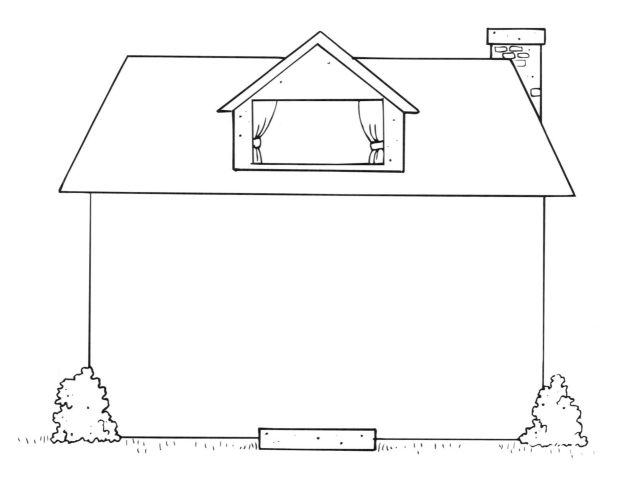

Read, Sing, and Play Along! Lullaby Songs

Directions: Select your favorite story and read it with an adult. Then, write  the name of the story in the box and draw a picture about the story on the cover.

My Favorites

Directions: Draw  and color a picture of each of your favorites.

toy

tv show

friend

food

Directions: Draw  your favorite toy in the back of the wagon. Color the wagon.

Directions: Mark an X on the pieces of clothing that are in the wrong place. Color the picture.

Directions: Everyone is special. Everyone is a star. Trace  the ☆ around each child and color the pictures.

Note to Parents: Discuss these pictures with your child. Have your child talk about what each person is doing.

Directions: Draw and color a picture inside each star that shows how you are special.

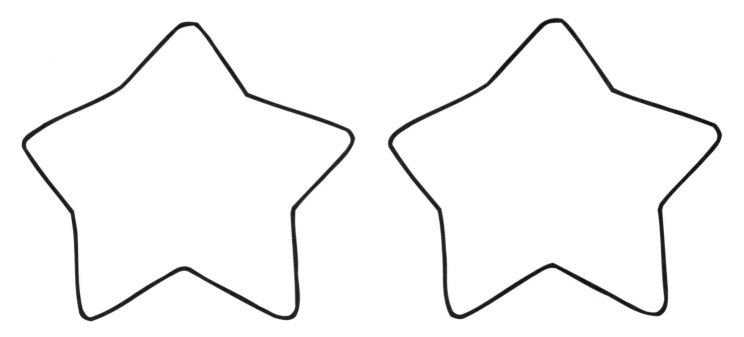

Directions: Color 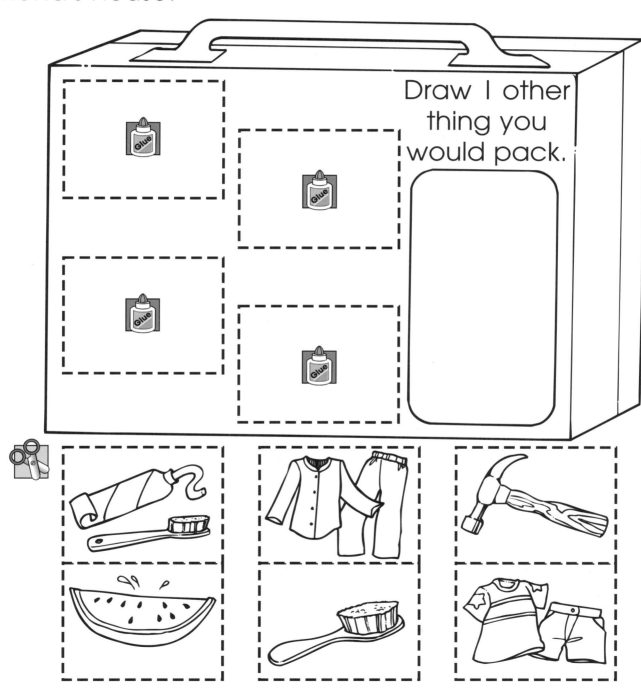, cut , and glue each thing that you might pack to sleep overnight at a friend's house.

Draw 1 other thing you would pack.

© 2006 School Specialty Publishing

Read, Sing, and Play Along! Lullaby Songs   **21**

Left blank for cutting activity
on previous page.

Name_____

Directions: Write  1, 2, or 3 in each ◯ to put the pictures in order. Color the pictures.

Note to Parents: Talk with your child about trips you have taken together. Look at photographs taken on those trips.

Directions: Draw  and color 🖍 a picture that shows the teddy bear what you want to be when you grow up.

What will you be?

Note to Parents: Explore different occupations with your child using books at home or at the public library. Many wonderful picture books are available. Talk with your child about what he or she might want to be.

Small to Tall

Directions: Color , cut, and glue the people in a row from small to tall.

Note to Parents: Before completing this page, encourage your child to put several different sized objects in order according to size.

Left blank for cutting activity
on previous page.

Exercise!

Directions: Circle  and color each child who is staying healthy by exercising.

Directions: Draw yourself in the picture doing your favorite activity for exercise.

Note to Parents: Before completing this page, talk with your child about the meaning of the word *exercise*. Give examples of different activities, and let your child decide if each one is a type of exercise. Take turns leading or following different exercises with your child.

Directions: Draw an X on the children who are wearing the wrong clothes. Circle and color the children who are wearing the right clothes.

Note to Parents: Talk with your child about the different types of weather and clothing choices that occur during different seasons.

Time to Sleep

Directions: Draw ✏️ a line from the pillow to each picture that shows how to rest to stay healthy.

© 2006 School Specialty Publishing

Read, Sing, and Play Along! Lullaby Songs   **29**

Name_____

Directions: It is fun to help shop for groceries. Draw an X  on each thing that is not a food item.

Directions:

Draw ✏ 4 yellow 🍌 s.

Draw ✏ 3 red 🍎 s.

Draw ✏ 2 orange 🍊 s.

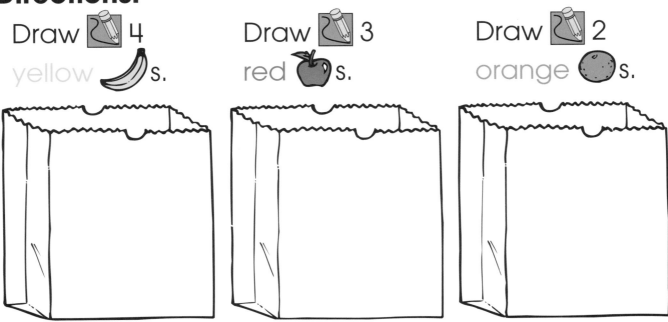

Note to Parents: Encourage your child to talk about his or her choices.

Healthful Foods

Directions: Color 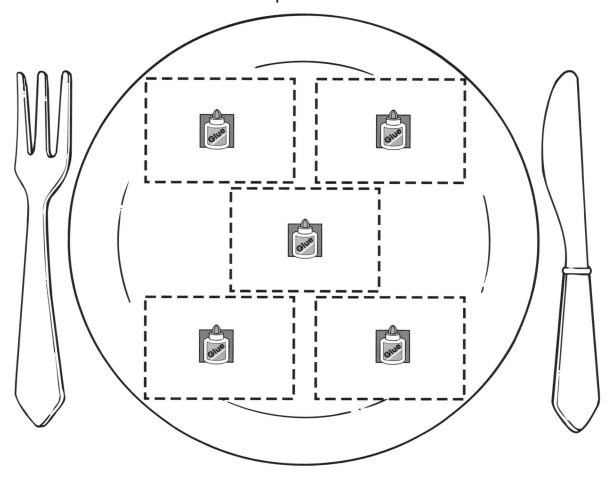, cut , and glue the healthful foods onto the plate.

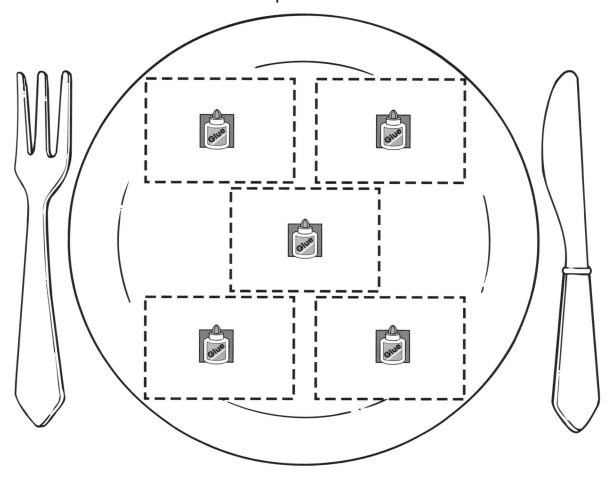

Note to Parents: Talk with your child about choosing healthful foods.

Left blank for cutting activity
on previous page.

What Comes Next?

Directions: Cut ✂ the pieces at the bottom of this page. Glue 🖊 the correct one in each empty space to complete each pattern.

Note to Parents: Have your child identify each picture aloud to determine what comes next in each pattern.

Left blank for cutting activity
on previous page.

Name_____

Directions: Write  the number 1, 2, or 3 in each box to put the pictures in order.

Note to Parents: Talk with your child about the sequence in the first set of pictures.

Directions: Circle and color each picture that shows how to take good care of your body.

Note to Parents: Talk with your child about healthful choices.

Do Not Eat

Directions: Mark an X 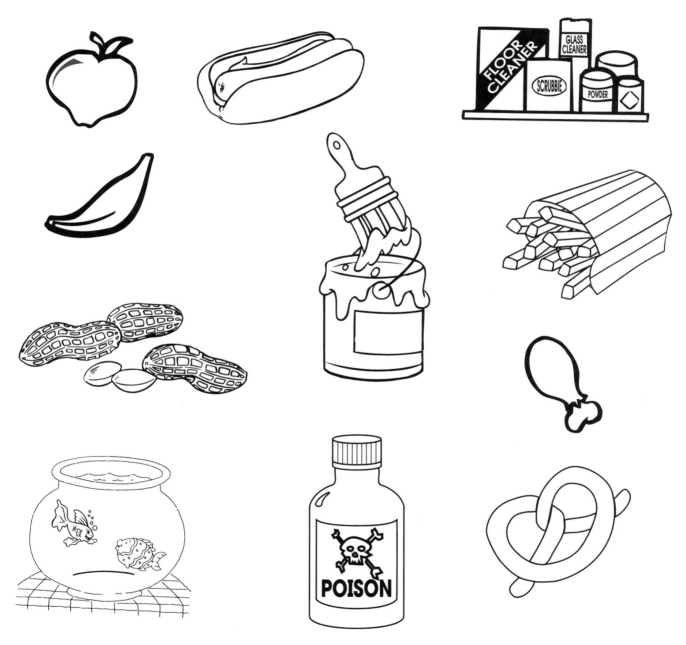 on things you should never eat. Color the safe choices.

Note to Parents: Talk with your child about making safe choices with food and nonfood items.

Read, Sing, and Play Along! Lullaby Songs **37**

Directions: Mark an X on items that are not safe to play with. Color items that are good choices.

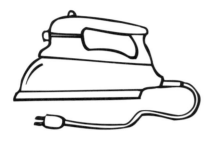

Note to Parents: Talk with your child about his or her choices.

In Case of Fire

Directions: Draw ✏️ a picture showing where your family will meet outside your home in case of a fire.

[ ]

This is our family meeting place.

Directions: Draw ✏️ two exits you can use from your room if there is a fire.

[ ]

Note to Parents: Talk with your child about fire safety. Practice how to get out of your house in case of a fire.

Name_____

Directions: Draw and color a picture of your family.

My last name is: _____.

Directions: Color the pictures that show what your family likes to do.

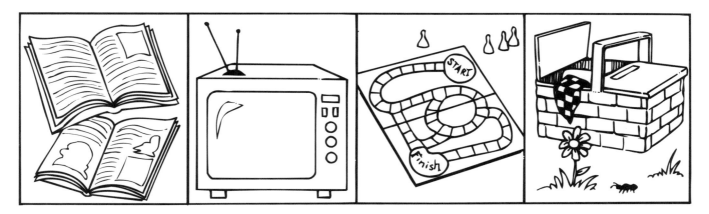

My Family

Directions: Write  the first name of each person in your family.

Ask your family to help you!

My Family Tree

Note to Parents: Help your child with the names and talk about the different relationships people have in your family (mother, wife, father, husband, son, brother, etc.).

Name_____

Directions: Draw 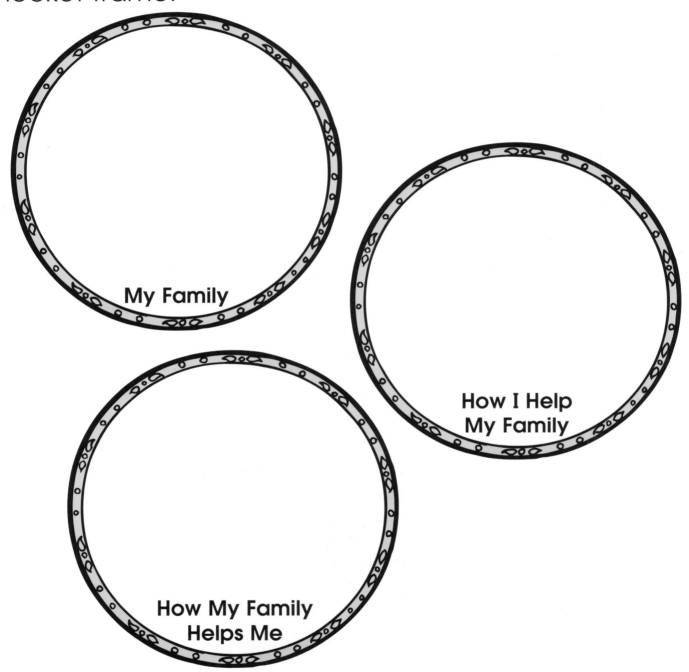 and color a picture in each locket frame.

My Family

How I Help
My Family

How My Family
Helps Me

Note to Parents: Discuss ways everyone in your family helps each other.

Visiting Grandparents

Directions: Grandparents are fun to visit. Draw 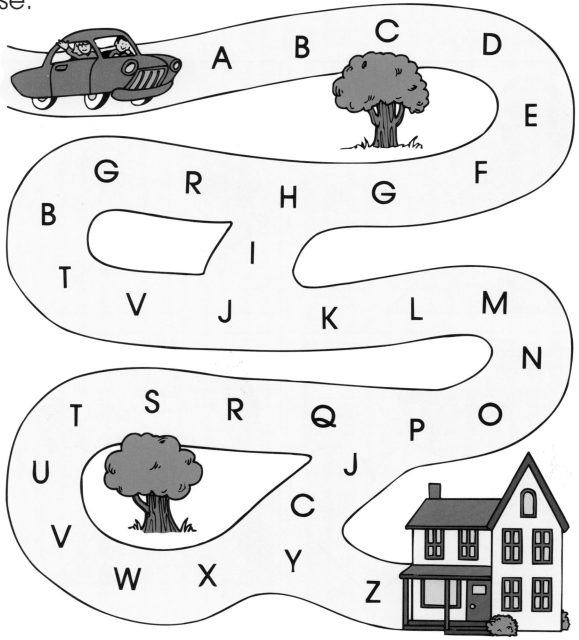 a line from A-Z to show the path to the grandparents' house.

Note to Parents: Before completing this page, sing the ABC song with your child.

Name_____

Directions: Color ✎ the ♡s red in each picture that shows how your family loves and cares for each other.

Note to Parents: Ask your child to describe what is happening in each picture.

Directions: Draw  a picture of something you and your family like to do together.

Note to Parents: Talk with your child about his or her drawing.

Name_____

Directions: Draw  a line from the baby to each picture that shows how to help care for the baby. Color the pictures.

Note to Parents: Ask your child to describe what is happening in each picture.

What Should You Do?

Directions: Circle  the picture that shows what each child should do. Color the picture you have chosen.

Note to Parents: Good character starts at home at a very early age. Discuss with your child what that means. Ask your child what he or she would do in different situations.

Clean Up!

Directions: Circle each thing in the bedroom that needs to be cleaned up.

Directions: Color the picture of the clean bedroom.

Name_____

Directions: Look at the ways you can help at home. Draw ✏ a line to match each picture with the things you would use to help.

Name_____

Directions: Sharing feels good. Count the things that are being shared. Write  the number in the ☐. Color the pictures.

Note to Parents: Give your child some examples of ways you have shared with others. Ask your child to tell you ways he or she has shared.

Honesty

Directions: Circle and color the picture that shows the boy or girl being honest.

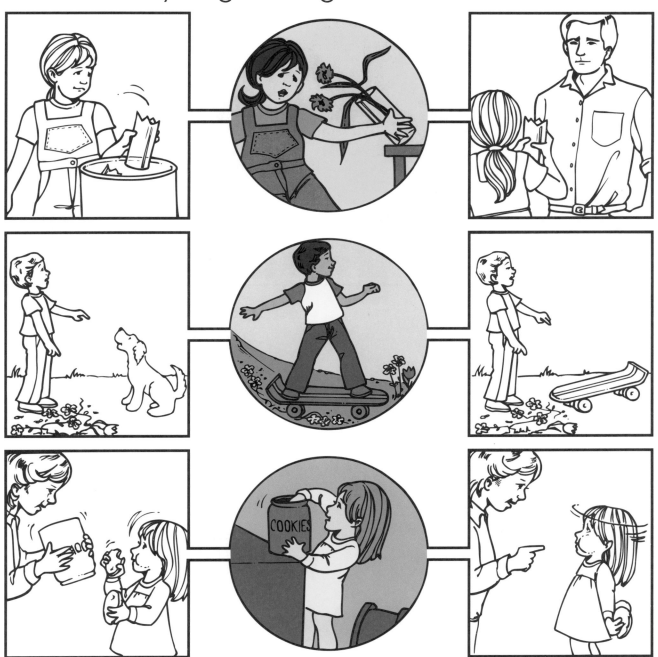

Note to Parents: Discuss with your child what it means to be honest.

Directions: Circle  each happy face in the crowd.

Directions:

Draw and color a happy face on the clown.

Note to Parents: Take turns with your child making faces that express different feelings. Try to guess what those feelings are.

Feelings

Directions: Draw 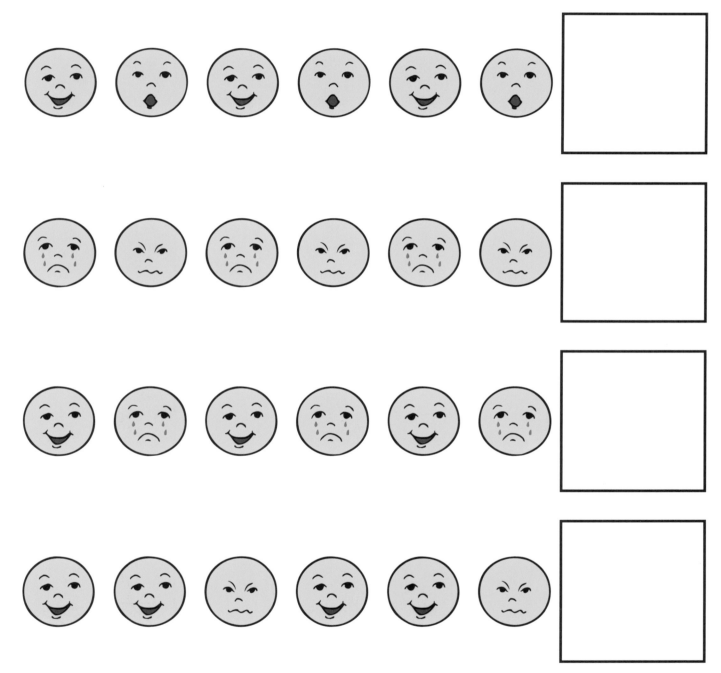 the next face to extend each pattern.

Note to Parents: Have your child describe each picture aloud to determine what comes next in the pattern.

Name _____

Directions: Draw a line to match the pictures that show why each child feels proud. Color the pictures.

Note to Parents: Talk with your child about what it means to feel proud.

Name_____

Directions: Look at each sad person. Draw a line from each sad picture to the picture that shows what makes each person happy.

Note to Parents: Ask your child to describe what is happening in each set of pictures.

Feelings

Directions: Look at the face beside each mirror. Draw 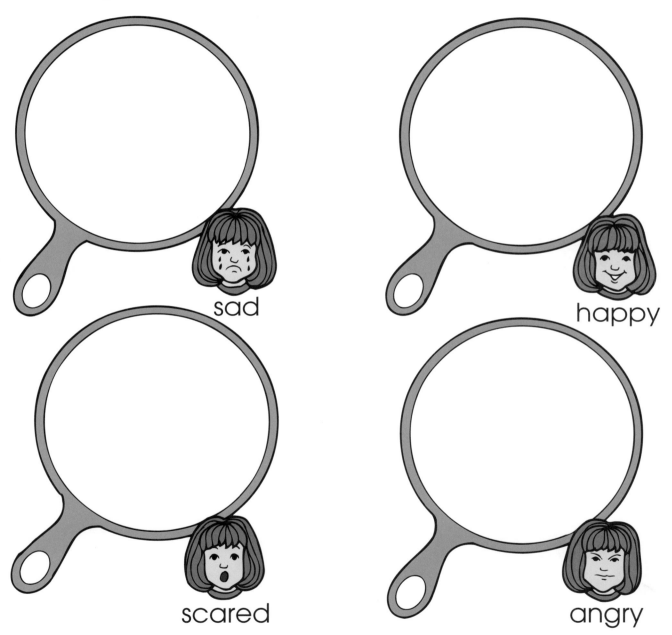 and color a picture in each mirror of something that would make you feel that way.

sad

happy

scared

angry

Note to Parents: Talk with your child about what makes him or her feel different emotions. Share your feelings.

Directions: Draw a face on the person in each picture to show how he or she might feel. Color the pictures.

Directions: Color ✏️ each picture that shows something that might scare you. Draw ✏️ a line to show what could make you feel safer in each situation.

Note to Parents: Talk with your child about what is scary to him or her.

Directions: Draw 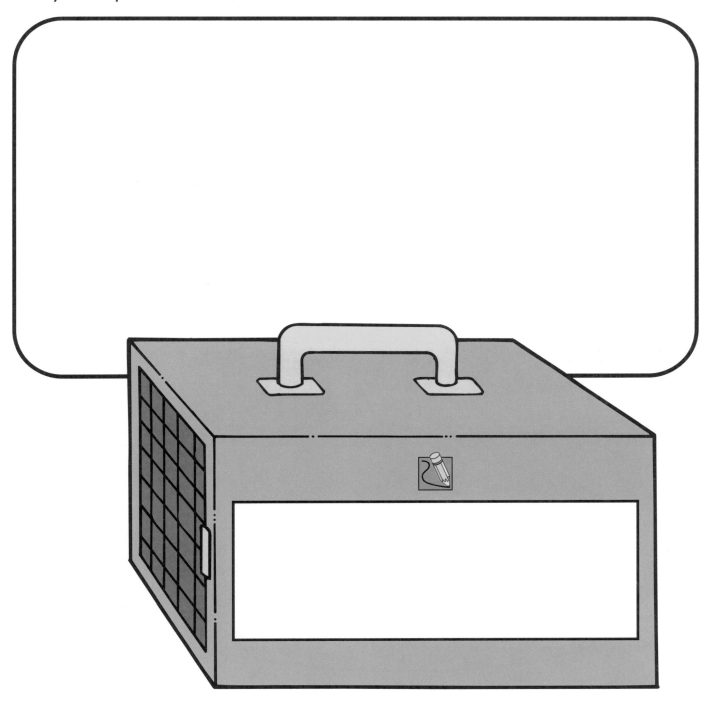 and color a picture of your pet or a pet you would like to have. Write the name of your pet on the carrier.

© 2006 School Specialty Publishing

Read, Sing, and Play Along! Lullaby Songs **59**

Name_____

Directions: Trace  the dotted lines from the cat to the box of kitty snacks.

Directions: Look at the pictures in each box.
Draw a line from each animal to its home.

Note to Parents: Talk with your child about different kinds of homes for different animals. Explore this topic at your public library.

Directions: Draw  a picture of you and a friend going to school. Dress you and your friend correctly for the weather. Write your school's name on the sign.

Note to Parents: Take your child to visit the school before the first day. Check to see if and when the school will be open so that you and your child may see the classroom and meet the teacher. Familiarity makes the transition to school easier.

Directions: Color 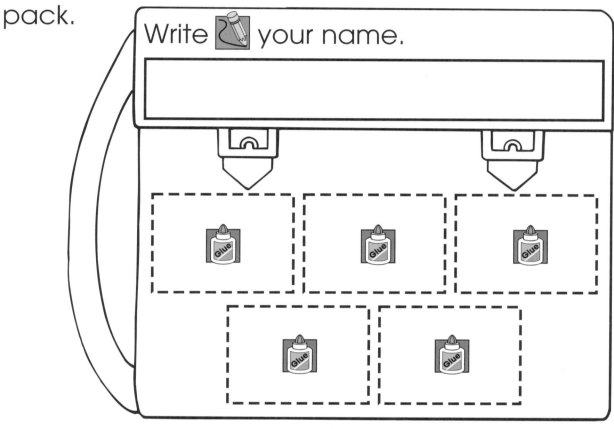, cut , and glue each thing you might pack for school inside the back pack.

Write your name.

Note to Parents: Talk with your child about supplies needed for school. Look at store school-supply sections or back-to-school sale flyers. Let your child cut out pictures of supplies and glue them to a blank piece of paper.

Left blank for cutting activity
on previous page.

Name_____

Directions: Inside the lunchbox, draw 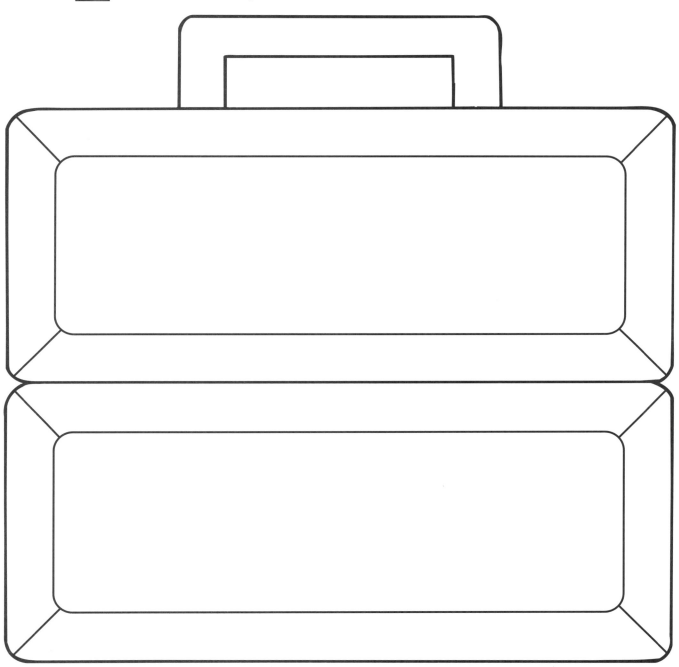 and color the foods you like to eat for lunch.

Note to Parents: Talk with your child about healthful lunch foods as well as your child's favorite lunch foods.

Directions: Color  the picture that shows how you will travel to school.

I will walk.

I will go in the car.

I will ride the bus.

Directions: Cut ✂ the pictures and glue 🅖 them to show what happened first, second, and third.

First
1

Second
2

Third
3

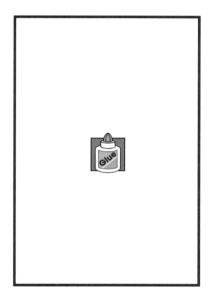

Left blank for cutting activity
on previous page.

Directions: Look at the pictures. What happened first? What happened second? What happened third? Draw a line from the correct word to the picture.

First
1

Second
2

Third
3

Note to Parents: Ask your child what he or she does first and last every day. What does he or she do in the middle of the day?

Name_____

Directions: Color  red the things that are going to the right. Color blue the things that are going to the left.

Note to Parents: Have your child identify his left hand and point to the left. Repeat with the right hand.

Going to School

Directions: Draw 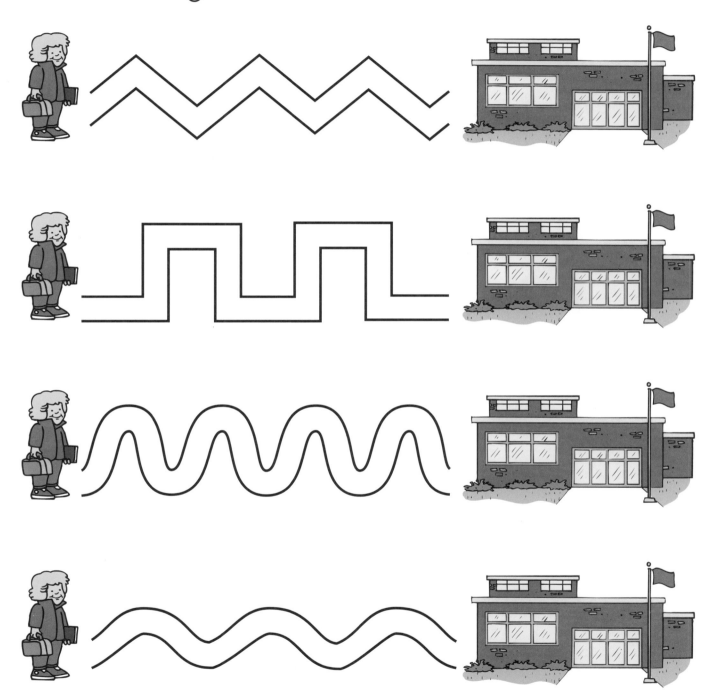 a line in each path to show the
child how to get to school.

Read, Sing, and Play Along! Lullaby Songs   **71**

My Teacher

Directions: Circle the teacher in each picture. Color your three favorite pictures that show how your teacher cares.

Note to Parents: Positive, enthusiastic comments about going to school help set the stage for a happy experience.

On the Playground

Directions: Draw an X  on each thing that does not belong on the playground.

Note to Parents: Talk to your child about favorite playground activities.

Be Good

Directions: In each circle, draw  either a ☺ for the children who are being good, or a ☹ for the children who are not being good.

Note to Parents: Talk with your child about good choices for behavior at school.

Name_____

Directions: Which pictures show things you can do at school? Color each if it has a school picture inside.

Note to Parents: Talk with your child about what he or she expects to do at school.

Name_____

Directions: Draw  a line from the friends in the center to each picture that shows how friends should act. Color the pictures of good friends.

Note to Parents: Talk with your child about being a good friend.

Name_____

Directions: Help the bear get to the honey. Follow the arrow to trace  a path to the honey.

Directions: Help the cow get to the grass. Follow the arrow to trace a path to the grass.

Above and Below

Directions: Color  the pictures **above** the clouds first. Then, color the pictures **below** the clouds.

Read, Sing, and Play Along! Lullaby Songs

Name_____

Directions: Trace  and color the cat that is **between** the other cats.

Directions: Color the mouse that is **between** the other mice.

Read, Sing, and Play Along! Lullaby Songs

Top, Middle, and Bottom

Directions: Color ✏ the **top** ball green. Color ✏ the **middle** ball yellow. Color ✏ the **bottom** ball red. Color ✏ the toys to show **top**, **middle**, and **bottom**. Use the same colors you used for the balls.

Directions: Draw ✏️ two apples **up** in the tree.
Draw ✏️ one apple **down** on the ground.

Directions: Draw 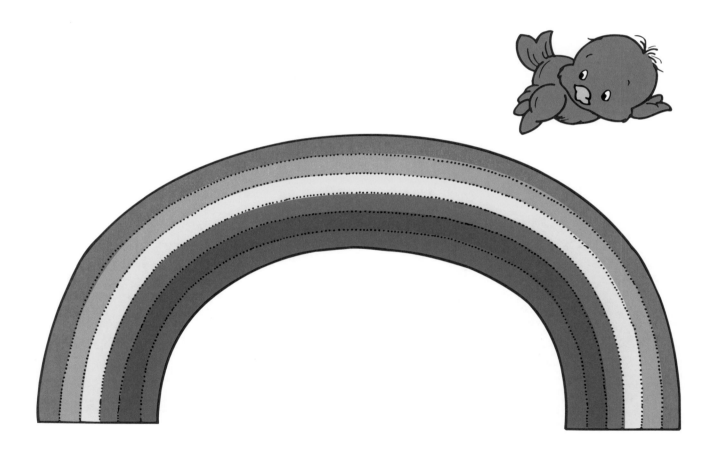 one bird flying **over** the rainbow. Draw another bird flying **under** the rainbow.

Directions:

Draw a dog on the **left**.

Draw a bug on the **right**.

Draw a frog on the **left**.

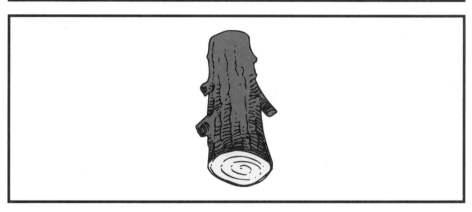

Draw a cat on the **right**.

Name_____

Directions: Look at the picture. Draw  some things that could be **inside** each one.

Answer Key

Youngest to Oldest

Name_____

Directions: Color the numbers 1, 2, and 3. Then, write the number 1, 2, or 3 in each box to put the pictures in order from youngest to oldest.

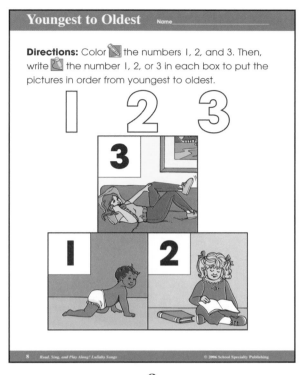

8

What Is Missing?

Name_____

Directions: Find and circle 10 things in the top picture that are not in the bottom picture.

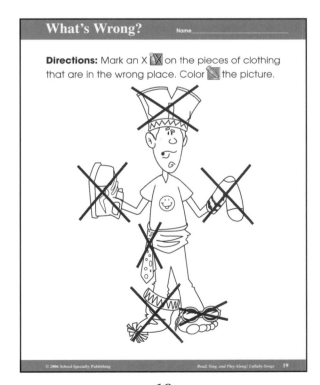

Note to Parents: Discuss all of the objects in the top picture. After completing the activity, if your child shows an interest, encourage him or her to list or draw the 10 items that are missing.

13

Color the House

Name_____

Note to Parents: Read the following directions one at a time to your child. Allow time for your child to complete each task before reading the next direction.

Directions: Color the roof brown.
Color the chimney red.
Color the bushes green.
Draw a front door. Color it blue.
Draw 2 windows beside the door.
Draw yourself looking out a window.
Draw flowers in front of the house.

15

What's Wrong?

Name_____

Directions: Mark an X on the pieces of clothing that are in the wrong place. Color the picture.

19

Answer Key

What Would You Pack?   Name_____

Directions: Color 🖍️, cut ✂️, and glue 📋 each thing that you might pack to sleep overnight at a friend's house.

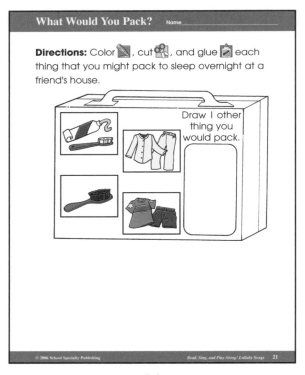

Draw 1 other thing you would pack.

21

Order   Name_____

Directions: Write 🖍️ 1, 2, or 3 in each ◯ to put the pictures in order. Color 🖍️ the pictures.

Note to Parents: Talk with your child about trips you have taken together. Look at photographs taken on those trips.

23

Small to Tall   Name_____

Directions: Color 🖍️, cut ✂️, and glue 📋 the people in a row from small to tall.

25

Exercise!   Name_____

Directions: Circle ⭕ and color 🖍️ each child who is staying healthy by exercising.

Directions: Draw yourself in the picture doing your favorite activity for exercise.

Note to Parents: Before completing this page, talk with your child about the meaning of the word *exercise*. Give examples of different activities, and let your child decide if each one is a type of exercise. Take turns leading or following different exercises with your child.

27

Answer Key

What's Wrong?

Name_____

Directions: Draw an X 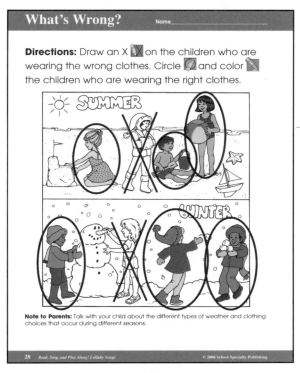 on the children who are wearing the wrong clothes. Circle and color the children who are wearing the right clothes.

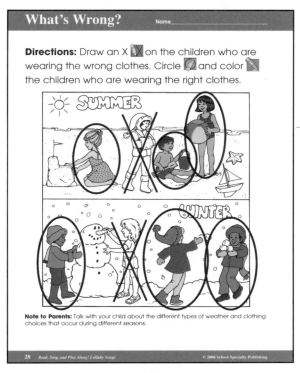

Note to Parents: Talk with your child about the different types of weather and clothing choices that occur during different seasons.

28

Time to Sleep

Name_____

Directions: Draw a line from the pillow to each picture that shows how to rest to stay healthy.

29

Healthful Foods

Name_____

Directions: It is fun to help shop for groceries. Draw an X on each thing that is not a food item.

Directions:

Draw 4 yellow s.   Draw 3 red s.   Draw 2 orange s.

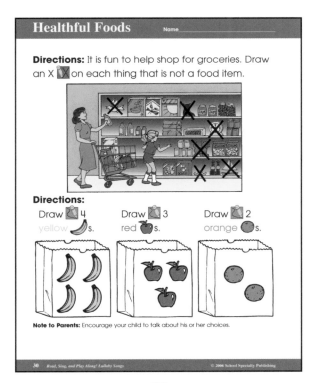

Note to Parents: Encourage your child to talk about his or her choices.

30

Healthful Foods

Name_____

Directions: Color, cut, and glue the healthful foods onto the plate.

31

Answer Key

What Comes Next? Name_____

Directions: Cut the pieces at the bottom of this page. Glue the correct one in each empty space to complete each pattern.

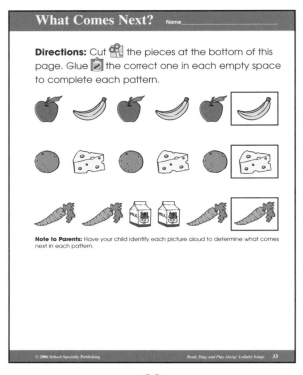

Note to Parents: Have your child identify each picture aloud to determine what comes next in each pattern.

33

Order Name_____

Directions: Write the number 1, 2, or 3 in each box to put the pictures in order.

Note to Parents: Talk with your child about the sequence in the first set of pictures.

35

Take Good Care of Yourself Name_____

Directions: Circle and color each picture that shows how to take good care of your body.

Note to Parents: Talk with your child about healthful choices.

36

Do Not Eat Name_____

Directions: Mark an X on things you should never eat. Color the safe choices.

Note to Parents: Talk with your child about making safe choices with food and nonfood items.

37

Answer Key

38

44

Visiting Grandparents   Name_____

Directions: Grandparents are fun to visit. Draw a line from A-Z to show the path to the grandparents' house.

43

Baby   Name_____

Directions: Draw a line from the baby to each picture that shows how to help care for the baby. Color the pictures.

Note to Parents: Ask your child to describe what is happening in each picture.

46

Answer Key

What Should You Do?   Name_____

Directions: Circle the picture that shows what each child should do. Color the picture you have chosen.

Note to Parents: Good character starts at home at a very early age. Discuss with your child what that means. Ask your child what he or she would do in different situations.

47

Clean Up!   Name_____

Directions: Circle each thing in the bedroom that needs to be cleaned up.

Directions: Color the picture of the clean bedroom.

48

Help at Home   Name_____

Directions: Look at the ways you can help at home. Draw a line to match each picture with the things you would use to help.

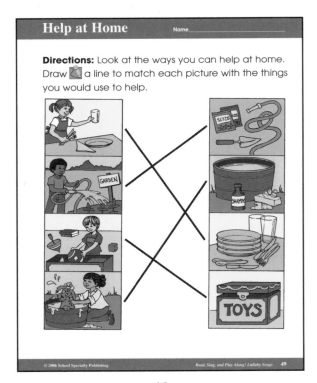

49

Sharing   Name_____

Directions: Sharing feels good. Count the things that are being shared. Write the number in the ☐. Color the pictures.

Note to Parents: Give your child some examples of ways you have shared with others. Ask your child to tell you ways he or she has shared.

50

Answer Key

51

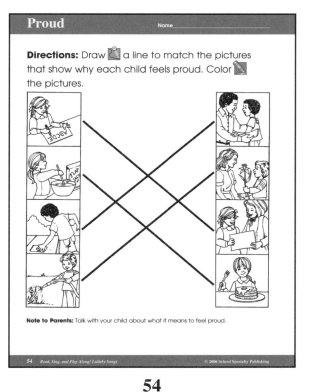

52

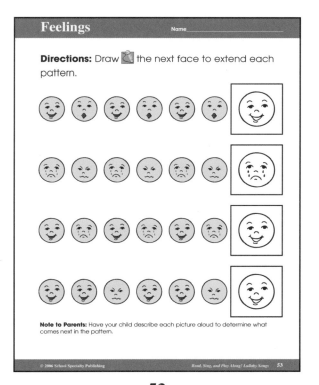

53

54

Answer Key

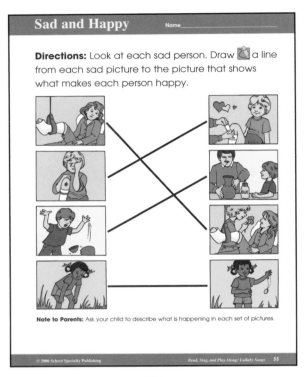

55

58

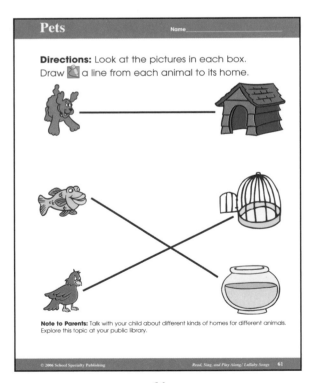

61

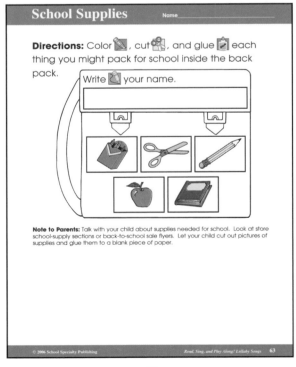

63

Answer Key

First, Second, Third   Name_____

Directions: Cut the pictures and glue them to show what happened first, second, and third.

First
1

Second
2

Third
3

67

First, Second, Third   Name_____

Directions: Look at the pictures. What happened first? What happened second? What happened third? Draw a line from the correct word to the picture.

First
1

Second
2

Third
3

Note to Parents: Ask your child what he or she does first and last every day. What does he or she do in the middle of the day?

69

Left and Right   Name_____

Directions: Color red the things that are going to the right. Color blue the things that are going to the left.

left   blue   red   right

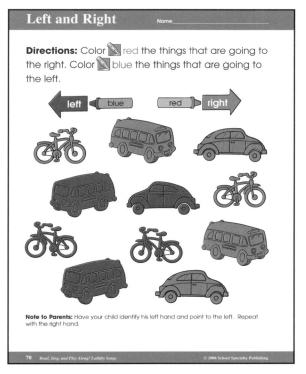

Note to Parents: Have your child identify his left hand and point to the left. Repeat with the right hand.

70

My Teacher   Name_____

Directions: Circle the teacher in each picture. Color your three favorite pictures that show how your teacher cares.

Note to Parents: Positive, enthusiastic comments about going to school help set the stage for a happy experience.

72

Answer Key

Directions: Draw an X 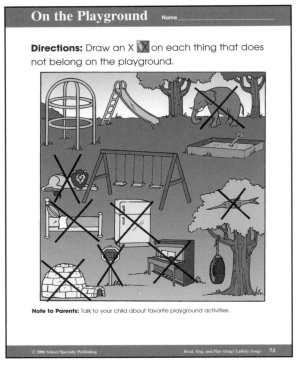 on each thing that does not belong on the playground.

Note to Parents: Talk to your child about favorite playground activities.

73

Be Good   Name

Directions: In each circle, draw either a ☺ for the children who are being good, or a ☹ for the children who are not being good.

Note to Parents: Talk with your child about good choices for behavior at school.

74

At School   Name

Directions: Which pictures show things you can do at school? Color each if it has a school picture inside.

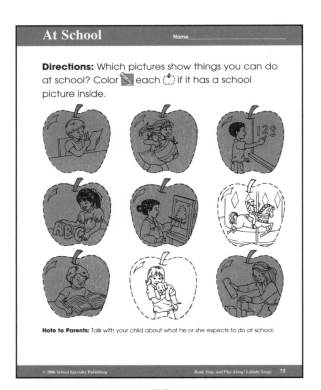

Note to Parents: Talk with your child about what he or she expects to do at school.

75

Friends   Name

Directions: Draw a line from the friends in the center to each picture that shows how friends should act. Color the pictures of good friends.

Note to Parents: Talk with your child about being a good friend.

76

Answer Key

Between   Name_____

Directions: Trace 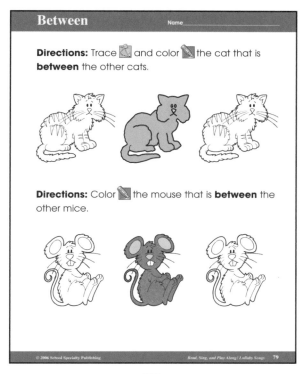 and color the cat that is **between** the other cats.

Directions: Color the mouse that is **between** the other mice.

   Read, Sing, and Play Along! Lullaby Songs   79

79

Top, Middle, and Bottom   Name_____

Directions: Color the **top** ball green. Color the **middle** ball yellow. Color the **bottom** ball red. Color the toys to show **top**, **middle**, and **bottom**. Use the same colors you used for the balls.

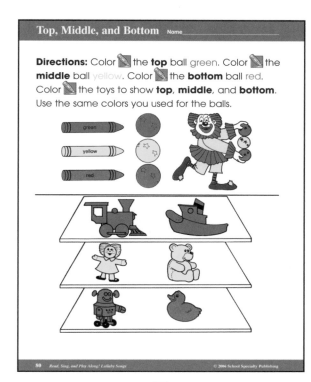

80

Up and Down   Name_____

Directions: Draw two apples **up** in the tree. Draw one apple **down** on the ground.

   Read, Sing, and Play Along! Lullaby Songs   81

81

Over and Under   Name_____

Directions: Draw one bird flying **over** the rainbow. Draw another bird flying **under** the rainbow.

82

   Read, Sing, and Play Along! Lullaby Songs   **95**

Answer Key

83

Stories and Finger Plays

© 2006 School Specialty Publishing

Read, Sing, and Play Along! Lullaby Songs **97**

The Big, Big Carrot

Things to do next.

Add It On!

Find six to ten carrots of various sizes. Encourage your child to line up the carrots from largest to smallest or from shortest to longest.

Be Silly!

Think of food dishes you could make if you had some carrots. Talk about what the recipes might be. For example, you could make a carrot sandwich, carrot soup, or carrot pudding! Use the plate on page 101 to draw your ideas!

Once upon a time, a girl planted a tiny carrot seed.

Soon, the seed sprouted. Every day, the girl watered it and watched as the green leaves grew bigger and bigger.

Her little sister wanted to help, but the girl said she was much too small to grow carrots.

One day, the girl went out to her garden to pull up the carrot. But try as she might, it was stuck too tight.

She called to her father, who was mowing the grass.

"Father dear, come here, come here. I've pulled with all my might. I can't pull my carrot out. It's stuck so very tight!"

So, the father came running. He grabbed on to the girl, and they both pulled and pulled, but the carrot was stuck too tight.

The father turned to the mother, who was hanging out the clothes.

"Mother dear, come here, come here. We've pulled with all our might. We can't pull this carrot out. It's stuck so very tight!" So, the mother came running. She grabbed on to the father, and they pulled and pulled, but the carrot wouldn't budge.

Next, the mother turned and called to the brother, who was riding around on his bike.

"Brother dear, come here, come here. We've pulled with all our might. We can't pull this carrot out. It's stuck so very tight!"

So, the brother came running. He grabbed on to the mother, and they all pulled and pulled, but the carrot wouldn't move an inch.

Next, the brother turned and called to the grandfather, who was washing the car.

"Grandfather dear, come here, come here. We've pulled with all our might. We can't pull this carrot out. It's stuck so very tight!"

So, the grandfather came running. He grabbed

Things to do next.

Be an Artist!

Paint with carrots! Wash several carrots. Cut them crosswise into thick rounds or lengthwise into halves. Let your child dip the carrots into paint and press them onto sheets of construction paper.

Brainstorm!

Think about the family members who helped the girl pull up the big carrot in the story. Ask your child questions about the members of your own family, such as "Who is the tallest? Who is the smallest? Who is the youngest?"

Food Fun!

Have your child help you wash some fresh carrots. Peel the carrots and serve them with a favorite dip.

Wiggle and Wriggle!

Pulling up the big carrot was hard work. Ask your child to show you his or her muscles. Talk about the things you need to do to grow safe, strong, and healthy. Then, have your child exaggerate pulling up the big, big carrot.

on to the brother, and they all pulled and pulled, but the carrot was still stuck tight.

Then, the grandfather turned and called to the little sister, who was playing with her wagon. "Baby dear, come here, come here. We've pulled with all our might. We can't pull this carrot out. It's stuck so very tight!"

So, the little sister came running. She grabbed onto the grandfather, and they all pulled and pulled—and out popped the carrot!

Everyone clapped for the little sister, because she turned out to be the greatest help of all. The carrot was so big that the girl was happy to let her little sister carry it to the house in her wagon.

Carrot Sandwich!

Think of some dishes you could make from carrots. Draw your ideas on the plate below.

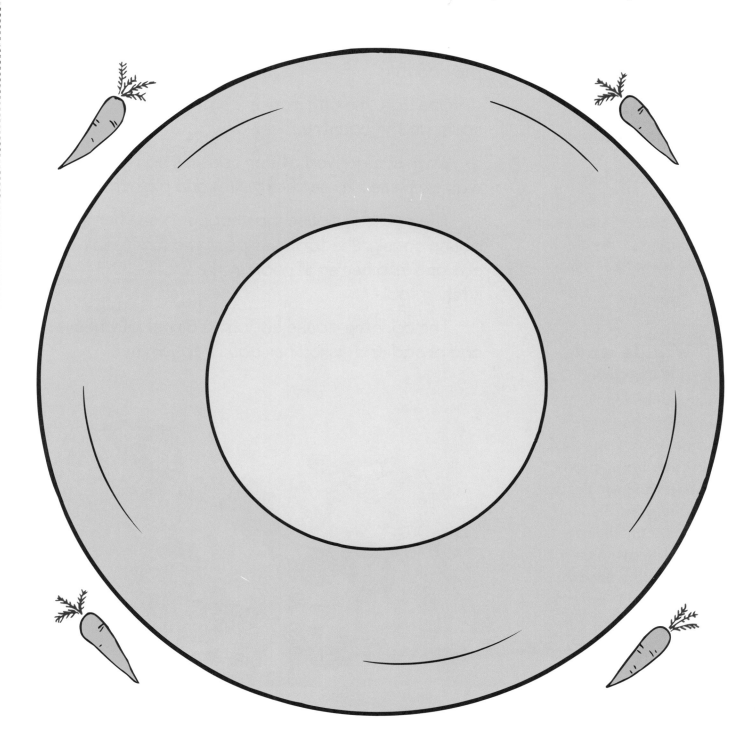

The Country Mouse and the City Mouse

Things to do next.

Be an Artist!

Cut out pictures of different types of houses from magazines. Give your child a large sheet of paper and some glue. Make a home collage! Ask which house your child would most like to live in and why.

Wiggle and Wriggle!

Ask your child to pretend to be a little mouse. Have your child show you how a mouse scampers and wiggles its nose and whiskers. Remind your child to be quiet in case a cat happens to be nearby.

Once upon a time, there were two mouse cousins. One lived in the city, and the other lived in the country.

One day, the city mouse went to visit her cousin in the country.

When she arrived at her cousin's house, she was surprised to see how small and plain it was.

The country mouse was happy to see her city-mouse cousin. She took her past the fat, sleeping cat and into her small room in the wall behind the kitchen table.

The country mouse set out a dinner of cheese and bread and asked her cousin to join her.

"Is this all you have to eat?" asked the city mouse. "How can you put up with such poor food? Come with me to the city. I will show you how to really live."

So, the two cousins set off down the road.

As they got closer and closer to the city, the traffic got heavier and heavier.

The country mouse held on tighter and tighter to her cousin's hand when they had to cross a street.

At last, they reached the city mouse's home. It was a beautiful, big house.

The city mouse led the way through a hole in the kitchen door and took the country mouse into a large dining room.

The table was covered with the remains of a feast.

Soon, the mice were filling up on pies, cakes, jellies, and other goodies. The country mouse thought it was all very grand.

Things to do next.

Can You Guess It?

Look through magazines or newspapers to find pictures of city items and pictures of country items. Cut out the pictures and let your child sort them into two groups, one for city life and one for country life.

Food Fun!

Make a mouse snack for your child. Cut several kinds of cheese into small squares. Serve with crackers. Encourage your child to eat the cheese like a mouse.

Tell your child you are going on a pretend trip either to the country or to the city. Put three or four small items in a suitcase. Let your child open the suitcase, look at the objects inside, and then close it. Repeat with your child, "I'm going on a trip, and I'm taking (name of objects)." See if your child can remember what items were in the suitcase. Make the game more challenging by adding more items!

Sound It Out!

The word *mouse* begins with the sound of the letter M. Ask your child to point out different objects in the room that begin with the sound of the letter M. When your child has found all of the objects in one room, move on to another!

Suddenly, they heard loud growling and barking. Two huge dogs ran into the room.

The city mouse cried, "Follow me!" Quickly, she ran across the table, down the table leg, and into a hole in the wall.

The country mouse followed as fast as she could, escaping the dogs by only a second.

The next day, the country mouse thanked her cousin for the visit but said that she was going home. As she left, the country mouse explained, "I would rather eat cheese and bread in peace than pies and cakes in fear."

Mouse Snacks

The city mouse and the country mouse are hungry.
Find the food items in the picture and color them yellow.
Then, color the rest of the picture!

Circle to show how many food items you colored.

 1   2   3   1   2   3   1   2   3   1   2   3

Read, Sing, and Play Along! Lullaby Songs

The Elves and the Shoemaker

Things to do next.

Add It On!

Line up several pairs of shoes. Help your child count the shoes one by one. Then, show your child how to count the shoes by twos. Ask your child which way of counting is faster, ones or twos.

Be an Artist!

Find an old pair of shoes that aren't worn very often. Give your child a large sheet of paper and some washable paint. Help your child dip the heel of the shoe into the paint and use it to create prints all over the paper!

Once there lived a very poor shoemaker and his wife. All they had was just enough leather to make one last pair of shoes.

The shoemaker cut out the leather for the shoes. Then, he and his wife went to bed.

In the morning, much to their surprise, they found the shoes already made and stitched to perfection.

The shoemaker's wife placed the shoes in their shop window and quickly sold them at top price.

With the money they received, the shoemaker bought enough leather to make two pairs of shoes.

He cut out the leather for the shoes in the evening. Then, he and his wife went to bed.

Again, when they awoke in the morning, they found the shoes already made and finely stitched.

The shoemaker's wife placed the two pairs of shoes in the shop window, and again, they were quickly bought by happy customers.

This time, the shoemaker had enough money to buy leather for four pairs of shoes.

Once more, he cut out the leather before bedtime, and again, the shoes were finished in the morning.

Soon, the shoemaker and his wife were no longer poor.

One evening, just before Christmas, the shoemaker and his wife decided to stay up all night to find out who was doing the good work. They set out a candle for light and hid behind a curtain.

At midnight, two little elves danced into the shop. They were poorly dressed, especially for wintertime, but they quickly set to work, hammering and tapping, sewing and snapping. By morning, all the shoes were finished, and the elves danced out the door.

The next day, the shoemaker and his wife decided to do something nice for the elves. The shoemaker set to work making them fine leather shoes. The shoemaker's wife spent all day making

Things to do next.

Be Silly!

Have your child pretend to wear different kinds of shoes. Ask your child to show you how to walk or dance in cowboy boots, galoshes, ballet slippers, athletic shoes, tap shoes, high heels, and thong sandals.

Can You Guess It?

Give your child the name of an occupation. Have your child guess what kind of shoes this person wears. For example, try a firefighter, ballerina, model, and a professional basketball player.

Things to do next.

Pretend!

Set up a play shoe store! Give your child a tape measure and several old pairs of shoes. Encourage your child to measure different family members' feet and find the pairs of shoes that fit them.

Wiggle and Wriggle!

Go outside on the sidewalk or find a hardwood or linoleum floor. Give your child a pair of shoes with a hard heel. Encourage your child to tap dance across the floor, moving as freely and creatively as possible.

them splendid pants and jackets.

That night, the shoemaker and his wife placed the tiny new shoes and clothes on the workbench and went to bed.

When the elves came, they were delighted with the gifts! They put on the new clothes, danced around the room once, and then danced out the door.

The elves never returned. But the shoemaker and his wife were never poor again, and they were always thankful for the help that the two elves had given them.

Busy Little Helpers!

What are the elves making? Connect the dots to find out.

© 2006 School Specialty Publishing

Read, Sing, and Play Along! Lullaby Songs **109**

The Gingerbread Boy

Once upon a time, there lived a farmer and his wife, who had no children.

One day, the farmer's wife was feeling very lonely. So, she decided to bake a gingerbread boy.

She mixed some gingerbread dough and then rolled it out gently. Next, she carefully cut out a large gingerbread boy.

She placed him on a cookie sheet, put him into the oven, and waited patiently for him to bake.

When she saw that the gingerbread boy was done, she opened the oven and took him out.

He was perfect. Now, she would no longer be lonely.

Then, much to her surprise, the gingerbread boy jumped off the cookie sheet and began running around the room.

The farmer's wife was thrilled. It was just like having a real child!

But when she tried to hold the gingerbread boy, he said, "Run, run, you can't catch me! I'm a gingerbread boy. I'm free. I'm free!"

Then, the gingerbread boy ran out the door.

The farmer's wife chased after the gingerbread boy, but he was too fast for her. He ran on and on to the field, where the farmer was working.

When the farmer tried to catch the gingerbread boy, he said, "Run, run, you can't catch me! I'm the gingerbread boy. I'm free. I'm free!"

Both the farmer and his wife chased after the gingerbread boy, but he was too fast for them.

He ran on and on past a cow, a pig, and a hen. They all tried to catch the gingerbread boy, but he was just too fast.

At last, the gingerbread boy came to a pond, where he had to stop. "Oh me, oh my," he said. "What shall I do now? I can't get wet."

Just then, out of the bushes stepped a sly fox. "Climb onto my back," the fox said. "I will give you a ride across the pond."

The gingerbread boy jumped onto the fox's back.

When they reached the middle of the pond, the

Things to do next.

Add It On!

Cut twenty gingerbread shapes out of paper or cardboard. Encourage your child to count all of the shapes. Then, sort them into groups of two, four, and five.

Be an Artist!

Give your child brown finger paint to use on a large sheet of paper. Encourage your child to paint a picture of the gingerbread boy. After the paint dries, give your child buttons, yarn, fabric scraps, and beads to decorate the picture!

fox lowered his back into the water. "Quick," he cried, "climb up onto my big nose! The water is deeper here."

The gingerbread boy quickly caught on to the sly fox's plan. Instead of climbing onto the fox's nose, where the fox would be able to easily gobble him up, the gingerbread boy hopped onto a rock and then onto the shore. He laughed at the angry fox. As he ran away, the fox heard him say, "Run, run, you can't catch me! I'm the gingerbread boy. I'm free, free, free!"

Brainstorm!

Talk with your child about why the gingerbread boy was afraid to cross the pond. Set out a bowl of water and some water-soluble and nonsoluble items, such as salt, pudding mix, a slice of bread, a carrot, a spoon, and a sheet of paper. Let your child pick an item, guess if it will dissolve or not, and place it in the water to find out!

Pretend!

Act out the story. Have your child be the gingerbread boy and pretend to be a small, round ball of dough. Encourage your child to lie flat as you roll over him or her with an imaginary rolling pin. After you pretend to bake the cookies, have your child move one arm, then the other, and then run away as you start to chase him or her.

Run, Run As Fast As You Can!

Color the spaces: 10—white ten—brown ⠿ ⠿—yellow

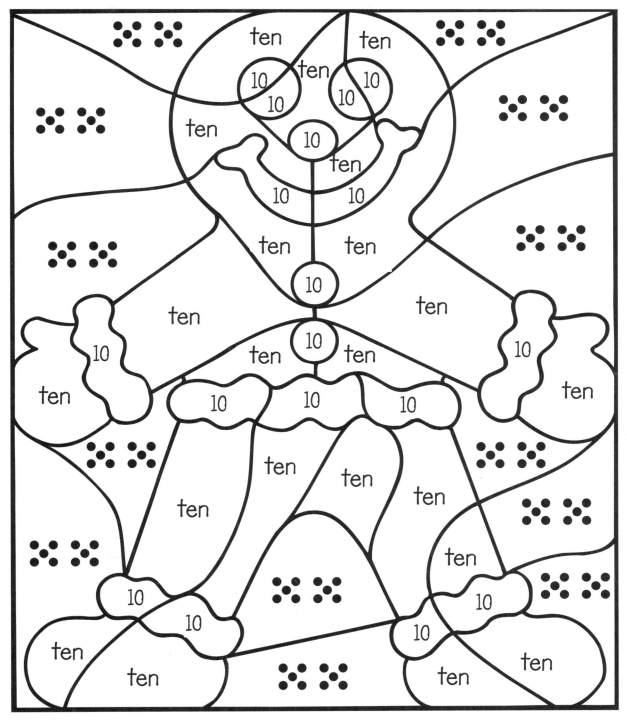

The Hare and the Tortoise

Once upon a time, there was a hare who liked to boast about how fast he could run.

One day, a tortoise heard the hare boasting, and she offered to race him.

"Sure," agreed the hare, as he laughed to himself. *I can easily outrun her*, he thought.

So, the hare and the tortoise decided where the race would begin and where it would end. Then, they asked an owl to be the referee.

When the hare and the tortoise were at the starting line, the owl said, "Ready, set, go!"

And off the two animals went.

Things to do next.

Be an Artist!

Make a turtle shell. Cut a hole for the head out of the bottom of a large brown paper bag and arm holes out of the sides of the bag. Let your child color the shell green or brown. Encourage your child to crawl like a turtle!

Be Silly!

Act out the story. Encourage your child to hop up and down whenever the hare is mentioned in the story and to crawl slowly on the floor whenever the tortoise is mentioned.

Soon, the hare was far ahead of the tortoise. In fact, he was so far ahead that he decided to stop for a short nap.

"That tortoise is so slow," he said. "Even if she catches up to me, I can easily run past her again."

The hare lay down and soon was fast asleep.

The tortoise crawled on and on. Eventually, she came to where the hare was sleeping.

"Oh my, he looks peaceful," she said. "It wouldn't be nice to wake him up." And she crawled on toward the finish line.

Things to do next.

Brainstorm!

Ask your child to finish these open-ended questions: When I go fast, I feel like _____. When I go slow, I feel like _____. Write your child's responses on a sheet of paper and let your child illustrate them!

Can You Guess It?

Talk with your child about things that go fast and things that go slow. Ask questions like, "Which is faster, a bike or a car? A jet plane or a scooter?" Then, ask, "Which is slower, a snail or a kitten? A bird or a worm?"

Sound It Out!

Hare is another word for *rabbit*, just like *tortoise* is another word for *turtle*. Brainstorm with your child different words he or she knows that begin with the sounds of the letters *R* or *T*.

Wiggle and Wriggle!

Play several different pieces of music, some with a fast tempo and some with a slow tempo. Encourage your child to hop like a rabbit for the fast music and to crawl like a turtle when a slow tune is played!

When the hare woke up, he looked all around. But he couldn't see the tortoise anywhere.

"That slow tortoise still hasn't caught up to me," he said.

But when the hare neared the end of the race, he got a surprise. There sat the tortoise, already on the finish line.

She was the winner!

After that day, the hare was not so boastful about how fast he could run. He had learned that being slow and steady can also win a race.

Fast and Slow

Fast and *slow* are *opposites*. Opposites are things that are different in every way. Draw a picture of the opposite below.

day

night

sad

happy

Henny Penny

Things to do next.

Add It On!

Put a variety of different kinds of nuts in a bowl. For example, use unshelled acorns, walnuts, almonds, peanuts, or pecans. Ask your child to sort the nuts by kind, size, color, or shape.

Be an Artist!

Make a leaf print. Give your child a sheet of paper, a crayon, and a leaf from an outside tree. Place the leaf under the paper and have your child rub the crayon across the paper until the leaf shape starts to show through.

One sunny autumn day, Henny Penny was walking down the road when—thump!—something fell on her head.

"Oh, dear me," said Henny Penny. "The sky is falling! I must go and tell the king." And off she ran.

Along the way, she met Ducky Lucky.

"Why are you running?" asked Ducky Lucky.

"I'm off to tell the king that the sky is falling!" said Henny Penny.

"Oh, dear me," said Ducky Lucky, grabbing his umbrella and holding it over his head. "May I come with you?"

"Yes," said Henny Penny. "But we must hurry."

So, Henny Penny and Ducky Lucky ran to tell the king that the sky was falling.

Along the way, they met Goosey Loosey.

"Why are you running?" asked Goosey Loosey.

"We're off to tell the king that the sky is falling!" said Henny Penny and Ducky Lucky.

"Oh, dear me," said Goosey Loosey, grabbing her old hat and putting it on her head. "May I come with you?"

"Yes," they said. "But we must hurry."

So, Henny Penny, Ducky Lucky, and Goosey Loosey ran to tell the king that the sky was falling.

Along the way, they met Turkey Lurkey.

"Why are you running?" asked Turkey Lurkey.

"We're off to tell the king that the sky is falling!" said Henny Penny, Ducky Lucky, and Goosey Loosey.

"Oh, dear me," said Turkey Lurkey, grabbing his three-legged stool and placing it on top of his head. "May I come with you?"

"Yes," they said. "But we must hurry."

Wiggle and Wriggle!

Talk with your child about gravity. Select a variety of objects for your child to hold up one at a time. Ask your child what will happen when he or she lets go of the object. Watch as the objects fall to the ground. Then, have your child jump into the air. Talk about why your child landed back on the ground.

Can You Guess It?

Set out a variety of different materials, such as a paper napkin, paper plate, cardboard square, aluminum foil, and piece of waxed paper. Encourage your child to touch and experiment with the materials. Have your child guess which materials would make the best protection from falling acorns!

Things to do next.

Food Fun!

Make peanut butter! Let your child help you shell a package of unsalted, roasted peanuts. Then, grind the peanuts in a food grinder. Mix the ground nuts with some softened margarine or butter and add salt for taste. (If your child is allergic to peanuts, make jelly instead by blending fresh berries.) Serve on crackers, apple slices, or celery sticks.

Sound It Out!

Point out to your child that all of the characters in the story have rhyming names, such as Henny Penny and Ducky Lucky. Add a rhyming word to your child's name to demonstrate the concept, for example Christy Misty. Then, do the rhyming activity on page 121.

So, Henny Penny, Ducky Lucky, Goosey Loosey, and Turkey Lurkey ran to tell the king that the sky was falling.

Just before they reached the king's palace, they stopped to rest.

"Henny Penny," her friends said, "why don't you cover your head, too?"

"Oh, it's not really necessary," said Henny Penny. "The sky just falls in little pieces, like this." And she held out the small piece of sky that had fallen on her head.

"That's not a piece of sky," said Ducky Lucky, Goosey Loosey, and Turkey Lurkey. "That's an acorn, you silly hen!"

The animals all had a good laugh when they realized what had happened. Then, they walked back home in the warm autumn sunshine.

Rhyme Time!

Think of a word that rhymes with each picture.
Draw a picture of that word in the box.

bug

frog

Jack and the Beanstalk

Things to do next.

Add It On!

Give your child a handful of dry beans. Encourage your child to count each bean one at a time as high as he or she can. Ask your child to arrange the beans in groups of twos, threes, fives, or tens and to count the number of groups that can be made.

Be an Artist!

Talk with your child about what the magic beanstalk must have looked like. Ask your child open-ended questions like "How was Jack able to climb the beanstalk? What did the beanstalk leaves look like? How would the beanstalk feel to touch?" Then, draw a picture of the beanstalk on page 125.

Once upon a time, there was a young boy named Jack. He lived with his mother, who was a widow. Being poor, they had hardly any money, but they did have a cow.

One day, Jack's mother told him to go to the market and sell their cow for money. On the way, he met a man.

"Hey, boy," the man said. "I will trade you my magic beans for that cow."

Jack looked at the beans. He thought magic beans were very special. "Sure!" he told the man.

When Jack brought the beans home, his mother became angry. "Beans!" she shouted. "What can we do with a few beans? We will starve." And she threw them out the window.

In the morning, Jack looked out the window. The magic beans had sprouted overnight. There stood a magnificent beanstalk. It was so tall, Jack could not see the top of it. Jack ran outside and began to climb.

At the top of the beanstalk, Jack saw a huge castle. Jack was hungry, so he knocked on the castle door. A woman answered.

"I am very hungry," Jack pleaded. "Please, could you spare any food?"

"Okay, come in. I can spare some food," said the woman. "But you must eat quickly. A giant lives here, and he loves to eat little children."

As Jack finished eating, he heard a loud booming voice. "Fee-fi-fo-fum, I smell the blood of a little man. Be he alive or be he dead, I'll grind his bones to make my bread."

Quickly, Jack hid. The woman gave the giant some breakfast. After he had eaten, she brought him his bag of gold to weigh. The giant weighed the gold and soon fell fast asleep.

Jack quietly crept over to the table, grabbed the gold, and dashed out of the castle and down the beanstalk. Jack's mother was overjoyed at the sight of the money.

The next day, Jack woke up very early. He was eager to climb the beanstalk and visit the castle again. When he knocked on the castle door, the same woman answered.

"Please," said Jack, "I am very thirsty. Could you spare a cup of water?"

"Okay, come in," replied the woman, "but you must drink it quickly. The giant is in a terrible mood. His bag of gold disappeared."

Just then, Jack heard, "Fee-fi-fo-fum, I smell the blood of a little man. Be he alive or be he dead, I'll grind his bones to make my bread."

Quickly, Jack hid just as before.

Again, the woman gave the giant some breakfast. After he finished eating, he ordered her to bring him his magic hen. "Lay!" he told the hen. After the hen had laid three golden eggs, the giant fell asleep.

Things to do next.

Wiggle and Wriggle!

Have your child pretend to climb up the magic beanstalk. Then, at the top, pretend that the giant is awake and is chasing after him or her. Encourage your child to climb down the imaginary beanstalk as quickly as possible.

Food Fun!

Serve your child green beans or lima beans at a meal. Ask your child to examine the beans and describe them to you. Does your child think they are magic beans?

Things to do next.

Be Silly!

Ask your child what he or she would do with magic beans. Would your child plant them? Would your child give them away? Or would your child maybe eat the beans? Think of the different magical powers that your child might receive after eating the magic beans!

Pretend!

Tell your child you are going to pretend to be giants. Stomp around the room. Talk about how different things would look if you were giant-sized. For example, a tree would look like a piece of broccoli, and a person would look like the size of an ant.

Silently, Jack tiptoed over to the table, grabbed the magic hen, and dashed out of the castle and down the beanstalk. His mother was thrilled with the magic hen.

The next day, Jack once again climbed the beanstalk. When he knocked on the castle door, the same woman answered.

"Go away. The giant is very angry. His magic hen disappeared," she said.

"I am very tired. Please, could you spare a little corner for me to rest in?" begged Jack.

"Okay, come in," she said. "But only for a little while."

Jack was resting when he heard, "Fee-fi-fo-fum, I smell the blood of a little man. Be he alive or be he dead, I'll grind his bones to make my bread."

Quickly, Jack hid.

The woman served the giant his breakfast. After he had eaten, she brought him his talking harp. The harp's beautiful music soon lulled the giant to sleep.

Jack quietly crept over to the table, grabbed the magic harp, and started to run away. But when he reached the door, the harp called out loudly, "Master, master!"

The giant woke up with a roar and chased after Jack. Jack scurried down the beanstalk, but the giant was right behind him. When he reached the bottom, Jack grabbed an ax and began to chop down the beanstalk. The beanstalk swayed from side to side. The giant swayed from side to side. Finally, the stalk fell to the ground, and the heavy giant fell along with it. The giant never bothered Jack again, and Jack and his mother lived happily ever after.

Beautiful Beanstalk

Draw a picture of the magic beanstalk in the box below!

© 2006 School Specialty Publishing

Read, Sing, and Play Along! Lullaby Songs **125**

Things to do next.

Add It On!

Draw three to five simple pictures of different events from the story on note cards. For example, draw wheat, the sack of flour, and the baked loaf of bread. Then, have your child arrange the cards in the order they happened in the story.

Be an Artist!

Cut a large sheet of paper in the shape of a slice of bread. Combine all-purpose flour with water to make a mixture the consistency of finger paint. Add some salt for texture. Let your child fingerpaint with the mixture on the paper!

Once upon a time, a little red hen was out in the barnyard with her friends.

She spotted a grain of wheat on the ground, and it gave her an idea.

"Who will help me plant this wheat?" she asked.

"Not I," said the duck.

"Not I," said the pig.

"Not I," said the cow.

"Then, I'll plant it myself," said the little red hen. And she did.

The grain of wheat sprouted and grew into a tall plant. Soon, it was yellow and ripe.

"Who will help me cut this wheat?" asked the little red hen.

"Not I," said the duck.

"Not I," said the pig.

"Not I," said the cow.

"Then, I'll cut it myself," said the little red hen. And she did.

When the wheat was cut, the little red hen asked, "Who will help me thresh this wheat?"

"Not I," said the duck.

"Not I," said the pig.

"Not I," said the cow.

"Then, I'll thresh it myself," said the little red hen. And she did.

When the wheat was ready to be ground into flour, the little red hen asked, "Who will help me grind this wheat?"

"Not I," said the duck.

"Not I," said the pig.

"Not I," said the cow.

"Then, I'll grind it myself," said the little red hen. And she did.

When the wheat was ground into flour, the little red hen asked, "Who will help me make some bread?"

"Not I," said the duck.

"Not I," said the pig.

"Not I," said the cow.

Things to do next.

Brainstorm!

The little red hen's babies are called *chicks*. Encourage your child to name the babies of the other farm animals mentioned in the story.

Food Fun!

Ask your child to help you make a simple muffin or bread recipe (or use a can of already mixed bread dough). Watch as the bread rises in the oven. When it's cooled, eat up!

Things to do next.

Sound It Out!

Find several pictures of different farm animals and set them facedown on a table. Have your child pick up a picture and make the sound of the animal on the card. Try to guess what animal it is. Then, switch roles. Let your child try to guess what animal noise you are making.

Wiggle and Wriggle!

Have your child pretend to be the little red hen in the story. Act out how she planted the wheat, cut it, threshed it, ground it, and baked it into bread!

"Then, I'll make it myself," said the little red hen. And she did.

When the bread was baked, the little red hen asked, "Who will help me eat this bread?"

"I will," said the duck.

"I will," said the pig.

"I will," said the cow.

"Did you help me plant and cut the wheat?" asked the little red hen.

"No," said the animals.

"Did you help me thresh and grind the wheat?" asked the little red hen.

"No," said the animals.

"Did you help me bake the bread?" asked the little red hen.

"No," said the animals.

"Then, you won't help me eat the bread," said the little red hen. "My chicks and I will eat it ourselves!"

And that is exactly what they did.

The Little Red Hen's Bread

Read the recipe to your child.
Then, have your child write **Yes** or **No** after each sentence.

Ingredients

2 cups flour

1 teaspoon salt

1 egg

1 cup milk

1. The little red hen uses 2 teaspoons of salt. _____

2. The little red hen uses 1 egg. _____

3. The little red hen uses 6 cups of milk. _____

4. The little red hen uses 2 cups of flour. _____

Little Red Riding Hood

Things to do next.

Add It On!

Set out a variety of baskets. Let your child line up the baskets from smallest to largest or from largest to smallest. Count how many baskets there are all together.

Be an Artist!

Give your child a large sheet of paper and some glue. Encourage your child to look through old magazines to find pictures of red items. Then, glue them to the paper to make a red collage!

Once upon a time, there was a little girl who always wore a red cape. Everyone called her Little Red Riding Hood.

One day, Little Red Riding Hood baked some bread for her sick grandmother. She put it into a basket with other goodies and set off on the path through the woods to her grandmother's house.

When she had gone halfway, Little Red Riding Hood met a wolf.

"Where are you going?" asked the wolf.

"To Grandmother's house," said Little Red Riding Hood. "It's on the other side of the woods."

"Well, I must not keep you," said the wolf. "Have a nice visit." And off he ran to Grandmother's house through a shortcut in the woods.

When Little Red Riding Hood arrived at her grandmother's house, she knocked on the door and said, "Grandmother, it's me, Little Red Riding Hood. I've brought you some fresh bread."

"Come in, my dear," called a deep voice.

Oh my, thought Little Red Riding Hood. *Grandma must be very sick to sound so bad.*

When Little Red Riding Hood went inside, she saw someone lying in bed. "Grandma," she exclaimed, "what big arms you have!"

"All the better to hug you with, my dear."

"But Grandma," said Little Red Riding Hood, "what big eyes you have!"

"All the better to see you with, my dear."

"But Grandma," said Little Red Riding Hood, "what big ears you have!"

"All the better to hear you with, my dear."

"But Grandma," said Little Red Riding Hood, "what big teeth you have!"

"All the better to eat you with!" cried the wolf, as he *jumped* up from the bed and grabbed Little Red Riding Hood.

Just then, the door flew open and in came a woodsman carrying his ax. The wolf let go of Little Red Riding Hood and ran out the door as fast as he could.

Little Red Riding Hood was very glad to see the woodsman. Together, they looked around the

Things to do next.

Brainstorm!

Little Red Riding Hood loved her Grandma very much. Talk with your child about grandparents or special people in his or her life that fit this role. Brainstorm ways that these individuals are special to your child.

Can You Guess It?

Experiment with your child's sense of taste. Select three different types of bread or crackers, such as white, rye, and wheat. Place bite-size pieces in separate baskets with a cloth or paper towel over the tops. See if your child can describe the pieces by taste!

Things to do next.

Food Fun!

Serve red foods to your child as a snack. Include things like apple slices, strawberries, tomatoes, red bell peppers, or cranberry juice. Serve them on a red placemat with a red paper napkin!

Pretend!

Find props to use for acting out the story, such as a red blanket or cape, a basket, a shawl for Grandma, and a pair of construction paper ears for the wolf. Act out different characters from the story!

house and soon found Little Red Riding Hood's grandmother safe and sound in the closet.

Grandmother made a pot of tea. Then, they all sat down and ate the bread and goodies that Little Red Riding Hood had brought.

Little Red Riding Hood had learned a lesson. Never again did she talk to strangers or walk alone through the woods.

Going to Grandma's House

Little Red Riding Hood is going to Grandmother's house.
Which is the **shorter** path? Color that path blue.
Color the **longer** path orange. Then, color the rest of the picture.

Rumpelstiltskin

Things to do next.

Add It On!

Try a simple weaving project with your child. Cut apart a brown paper grocery bag so it lays flat. Punch a row of equally spaced holes across it. Knot a piece of yarn at one end. Help your child weave the yarn up and down through the holes in the paper in a sewing-like style.

Be an Artist!

Have your child illustrate his or her favorite scene from the story on a sheet of paper, using gold crayons or markers.

Once upon a time, there was a miller. He was very poor, but he had a beautiful daughter. One day, he saw the king. The miller wanted to say something important to the king, but he couldn't think of anything to say. So, he lied. The miller said, "I have a daughter who can spin straw into gold."

The king thought that was amazing. He ordered the miller to send his daughter to his palace at once.

When the girl reached the palace, the king put her in a room full of straw, gave her a spinning wheel, and told her to spin all of the straw into gold by morning or she would be punished. Then, he locked the door and left.

The miller's daughter cried. She had no idea how to spin straw into gold. Suddenly, the door opened, and a strange little man walked in. "Good evening," he said. "Why are you crying?"

"The king said I must spin all of this straw into gold," sobbed the girl, "and I don't know how to do it!"

"What will you give me if I do it for you?" asked the little man.

"I will give you my necklace," said the miller's daughter. The little man went to work. Before morning, he had spun all of the straw into gold.

The king was pleased with what he saw, but it only made him greedier.

That night, he put the miller's daughter into a larger room full of straw. He told her to spin all of the straw into gold or she would be punished.

The miller's daughter was sad and afraid. She didn't know how to spin straw into gold. She began to cry.

Suddenly, the little man appeared again. He said, "What will you give me if I spin this straw into gold for you?"

"My ring," answered the miller's daughter. The little man set to work. By morning, he had spun all the straw into glittering gold.

The king was overjoyed at the sight of all the gold, but still he wanted more. He put the miller's daughter into a larger room full of straw. He told her that if she spun all of the straw into gold before the morning, he would marry her and make her the queen.

Again, the miller's daughter was sad and frightened. She didn't know how to spin straw into gold. She began to cry. Suddenly, the little man appeared again. He asked, "What will you give me if I spin this straw into gold for you?"

"I have nothing left to give you," answered the miller's daughter.

"Then, promise me that if you become queen, you will give me your first child," said the little man.

The miller's daughter agreed. The little man went to work and spent the whole night spinning the straw into gold. Then, he left.

When the king found the gold, he married the miller's daughter immediately. A year later, the queen had a child. The queen was in her room, rocking her baby to sleep, when the little man walked into the room.

"Good evening, Queen," he said. "I have come for what you promised me."

"Oh, no," cried the queen. "Don't take my baby." And she began to cry.

Things to do next.

Can You Guess It?

Think of a first name. Have your child try to guess what name you are thinking of. Give your child hints like "It starts with the sound of the letter S" or "The name of your favorite friend."

Pretend!

Make a crown out of sturdy paper and aluminum foil. Help your child decorate the crown with buttons, fabric scraps, or stickers. Then, let your child be king or queen for the day!

Things to do next.

Sound It Out!

Rumpelstiltskin is an interesting and unusual name. Brainstorm with your child other names that begin with the sound of the letter R. Write these names on page 137

Wiggle and Wriggle!

Pretend to be Rumpelstiltskin, dancing around the fire. Repeat with your child, "The queen will never guess the game, that Rumpelstiltskin is my name!" Dance as wildly and as silly as possible!.

"Don't cry," said the little man. "I'll give you a chance to keep your baby. If you can guess my name within the next three days, I will leave you in peace with your baby. I'll come back each night and give you a chance to guess my name. If you don't guess it, the baby is mine."

After the little man left, the queen asked her messenger to get her a list of all the names in her kingdom. When the little man returned that evening, the queen read him the list of names.

"Not one of those is my name," laughed the little man as he left.

The next day, the queen got a new list of names. When the little man appeared, she read him the list.

"Not one of those is my name," said the little man. "You have one more chance." Then, he left.

The queen asked her messenger for another list of names. When the messenger returned, he said, "I couldn't find any more names, but I did see something strange. I saw a little man dancing around a fire. As he danced, he sang,

"Today I brew, tomorrow I bake. Tomorrow night, the queen's baby I take! For the queen will never guess the game, that RUMPELSTILTSKIN is my name!"

The queen was very happy to hear the little man's name! That evening, when the little man appeared in her room, he   said, "Good evening, Queen. Can you guess my name?"

"Hmmm," said the queen. "Is it Bill or Conrad or Harry?"

"No!" said the little man, laughing.

"Well, then, is it . . . Rumpelstiltskin?" asked the queen.

"Who told you?" howled the little man. Then, he stomped and stomped around the room. He stomped so hard that he made a big hole in the floor and fell in! The queen and her baby never saw the little man again.

What's That Name?

Think of some other names that begin with the sound of the letter R.
Write them below!

Name List

Stone Soup

Things to do next.

Add It On!

Give your child stones of different sizes. Let your child sort the stones by size, shape, or color.

Be an Artist!

Draw the shape of a large pot on a sheet of paper. Have your child fill the pot by drawing the ingredients from the story.

Once upon a time, a beggar came to a small village. He went from door to door asking for food.

Everywhere he went, people complained that they were too poor and did not have any food to share.

The beggar said that he was sorry the village was so short of food and that if the people would lend him a large pot, he would show them how to make stone soup.

All the villagers gathered around because they wanted to learn how to make soup from a stone.

One of the villagers ran off and came back carrying a large pot. He helped the beggar fill the pot with water and place it over a hot fire.

The beggar then searched the village grounds until he found a stone that was just the right size. He washed the stone until it was clean and dropped it into the pot of water.

Another villager brought him a big spoon, and the beggar began to stir the soup.

Stir, stir, sniff, sniff.

"Mmm," he said. "This soup is going to be very good, but it would be even better if it had a

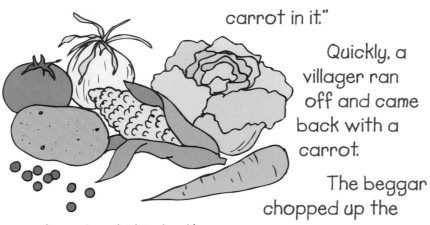

carrot in it."

Quickly, a villager ran off and came back with a carrot.

The beggar chopped up the carrot and put it into the soup.

Stir, stir, sniff, sniff.

"Mmm," he said. "This soup is going to be very good, but it would be even better if it had a potato in it."

Quickly, a villager ran off and came back with a potato.

The beggar chopped up the potato and put it into the soup.

Stir, stir, sniff, sniff.

"Mmm," he said. "This soup is going to be very good, but it would be even better if it had a tomato in it."

Quickly, a villager ran off and came back with a tomato.

The beggar chopped up the tomato and put it into the soup.

Stir, stir, sniff, sniff.

"Mmm," he said. "This soup is going to be very good, but it would be even better if it had an onion in it."

Things to do next.

Brainstorm!

Brainstorm with your child as many different kinds of soup as possible. Invent new kinds of soup by combining the names of different vegetables.

Be Silly!

Make a vegetable person using the vegetables you have in your kitchen. For example, your child might use a tomato for a head, a potato for the body, and carrot sticks for arms and legs. Use toothpicks to hold the different body parts together. Encourage your child to experiment and make as many silly variations as possible!

Things to do next.

Food Fun!

Make your very own stone soup! Find a large, flat stone, scrub it clean, and boil it in a pan of water. Then, add it to a larger pan full of water. Let your child add vegetables, such as carrots, potatoes, and onions, and powdered broth. Bring the soup to a slow boil. When the vegetables are tender, let the soup cool. Sieve out the stone before serving the soup. Then, do the activity on page 141.

Wiggle and Wriggle!

Take your child on a stone-hunting adventure! Go outside for a walk and bring along a plastic bag. Encourage your child to collect rocks of all different shapes and sizes.

Quickly, a villager ran off and came back with an onion.

The beggar chopped up the onion and put it into the soup.

Stir, stir, sniff, sniff.

"Mmm," he said. "This soup is going to be very good, but it would be even better if it had some broth in it."

Quickly, a villager ran off and came back with some broth.

The beggar added the broth to the soup.

Stir, stir, sniff, sniff.

"Mmm," he said. "My stone soup is done. Now, I will share it with all of you."

Everyone in the village was amazed that the beggar was so generous.

He shared his soup. He shared his recipe.

"We owe him a lot," said the villagers.

And from that day on, they never again let a beggar go hungry from their village.

Hot Soup!

Color a path from the vegetables to the pot of stone soup.

There Was an Old Woman Who Swallowed a Fly

Things to do next.

Add It On!

Add sound effects to the story! Think of simple sound effects for each character in the story. For example, when the fly is mentioned, have your child make a buzzing sound. When the cat is mentioned, ask your child to meow.

Brainstorm!

Insects fascinate children. Take advantage of this curiosity by helping your child collect four or five different bugs, including a fly. Catch them in jars to notice and compare their different features, such as legs, antennae, wings, and eyes. When you're finished observing, be sure to set them free again!

There was an old woman who swallowed a fly. I don't know why she swallowed a fly. Perhaps she'll die.

There was an old woman who swallowed a spider that wiggled and wriggled and jiggled inside her. She swallowed the spider to catch the fly. I don't know why she swallowed a fly. Perhaps she'll die.

There was an old woman who swallowed a bird. My, how absurd to swallow a bird! She swallowed the bird to catch the spider that wiggled and wriggled and jiggled inside her. She swallowed the spider to catch the fly. I don't know why she swallowed a fly. Perhaps she'll die.

There was an old woman who swallowed a cat. Imagine that, she swallowed a cat! She swallowed the cat to catch the bird. She swallowed the bird to catch the spider that wiggled and wriggled and jiggled inside her. She swallowed the spider to catch the fly. I don't know why she swallowed a fly. Perhaps she'll die.

There was an old woman who swallowed a dog. Oh, what a hog to swallow a dog! She swallowed the dog to catch the cat. She swallowed the cat to catch the bird. She swallowed the bird to catch the spider that wiggled and wriggled and jiggled inside her. She swallowed the spider to catch the fly. I don't know why she swallowed a fly. Perhaps she'll die.

There was an old woman who swallowed a goat. Just opened her throat and swallowed a goat! She swallowed the goat to catch the dog. She swallowed the dog to catch the cat. She swallowed the cat to catch the bird. She swallowed the bird to catch the spider that wiggled and wriggled and jiggled inside her. She swallowed the spider to catch the fly. I don't know why she swallowed a fly. Perhaps she'll die.

Things to do next.

Be an Artist!

Illustrate the story. Have your child draw a picture of what he or she thinks the old woman looks like on page 145.

Be Silly!

Think of additional things the old woman could have swallowed. For example, she could have swallowed a dog-catcher to catch the dog. Be as silly as possible!

© 2006 School Specialty Publishing

Read, Sing, and Play Along! Lullaby Songs **143**

Things to do next.

Can You Guess It?

Pick one of the animals from the story and act it out. See if your child can guess which animal you're pretending to be. Then, switch roles and let your child act while you guess.

Wiggle and Wriggle!

Have your child act out the story as you repeat it. Encourage your child to exaggerate swallowing all of the different animals, feeling sicker and sicker with each addition!

There was an old woman who swallowed a cow. I don't know how she swallowed a cow! She swallowed the cow to catch the goat. She swallowed the goat to catch the dog. She swallowed the dog to catch the cat. She swallowed the cat to catch the bird. She swallowed the bird to catch the spider that wiggled and wriggled and jiggled inside her. She swallowed the spider to catch the fly. I don't know why she swallowed a fly. Perhaps she'll die.

There was an old woman who swallowed a horse. She died, of course!

A Full Belly!

The old woman had a full belly. Draw a picture of all the things she swallowed below.

This Is the House That Jack Built

Things to do next.

Add It On!

Make up additional verses to the story with your child. For example, "This is the wolf that chased the cock that crowed in the morn." See how many verses you can create!

Be an Artist!

Ask your child what Jack's house looks like. Have your child illustrate it on page 149.

This is the house that Jack built.

This is the grain that lay in the house that Jack built.

This is the rat that ate the grain that lay in the house that Jack built.

This is the cat that chased the rat that ate the grain that lay in the house that Jack built.

This is the dog that worried the cat that chased the rat that ate the grain that lay in the house that Jack built.

This is the cow with the crumpled horn that tossed the dog that worried the cat that chased the rat that ate the grain that lay in the house that Jack built.

This is the maid all forlorn that milked the cow with the crumpled horn that tossed the dog that worried the cat that chased the rat that ate the grain that lay in the house that Jack built.

This is the man all tattered and torn that kissed the maid all forlorn that milked the cow with the crumpled horn that tossed the dog that worried the cat that chased the rat that ate the grain that lay in the house that Jack built.

This is the priest all shaven and shorn that married the man all tattered and torn that kissed the maid all forlorn that milked the cow with the crumpled horn that tossed the dog that worried the cat that chased the rat that ate the grain that lay in the house that Jack built.

Things to do next.

Food Fun!

Build a food house! Give your child stalks of celery, carrot sticks, or crackers. Use peanut butter to hold the pieces together. When your child is finished building, eat the creation!

Pretend!

Encourage your child to pretend to be Jack, building his house. Give your child plastic tools to use as props.

Things to do next.

Sound It Out!

Decorate a shoe box to look like a house. Find magazine pictures of different objects, many of which begin with the sound of the letter *H*. Have your child go through the stack of pictures and drop the ones that begin with the sound of the letter *H* into the house.

Wiggle and Wriggle!

Have your child build a house out of blocks or empty plastic containers. Make it as tall, wide, or big as possible!.

This is the cock that crowed in the morn that waked the priest all shaven and shorn that married the man all tattered and torn that kissed the maid all forlorn that milked the cow with the crumpled horn that tossed the dog that worried the cat that chased the rat that ate the grain that lay in the house that *Jack* built.

Jack's House

Draw a picture of Jack's house in the space below!

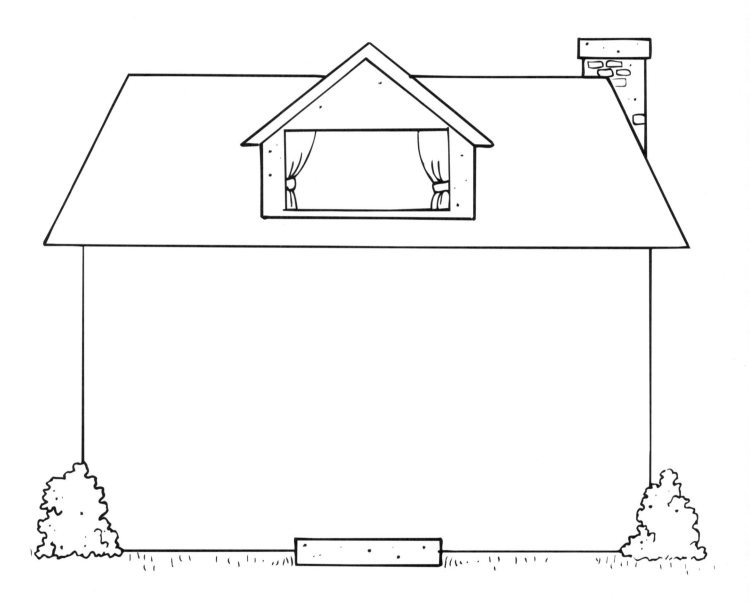

The Three Bears

Things to do next.

Add It On!

Gather three teddy bears (or other stuffed animals) of different sizes. In a pile, put different objects with varying sizes. You could use small, medium, and large plates, bowls, cups, or napkins. Encourage your child to match each object with the same-sized bear. For example, the large bear should get the biggest cup.

Be an Artist!

Make bear puppets! Give your child three small paper lunch bags and some crayons. Help your child draw faces on the bags to make a baby bear, mama bear, and pappa bear puppet. Use the puppets to act out the story.

Once upon a time, there were three bears—Papa Bear, Mama Bear, and Baby Bear. They lived together in a cottage in the woods.

One day, Mama Bear made some porridge for breakfast. The porridge was too hot to eat, so the bears went for a walk in the woods while it cooled.

While they were gone, a little girl named Goldilocks walked by their cottage and peeked inside. She saw the porridge on the table.

Goldilocks was very hungry, so she went into the cottage to taste the porridge.

First, she tried the porridge in Papa Bear's large bowl, but it was too hot.

Next, she tried the porridge in Mama Bear's medium-sized bowl, but it was too cold.

Finally, she tried the porridge in Baby Bear's small bowl, and it was just right. So, she ate it all up.

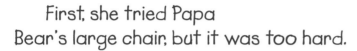

Then, Goldilocks decided to sit down and rest.

First, she tried Papa Bear's large chair, but it was too hard.

Next, she tried Mama Bear's medium-sized chair, but it was too soft.

Finally, she tried Baby Bear's small chair, and it was just right. So, she sat down.

But Goldilocks was too heavy, and the little chair broke all to pieces.

Then, Goldilocks decided to go into the bedroom and take a nap.

First, she tried Papa Bear's large bed, but it was too high.

Next, she tried Mama Bear's medium-sized bed, but it was too low.

Finally, she tried Baby Bear's small bed, and it was just right. So, she lay down and fell asleep.

After a while, the three bears returned from their walk.

"Someone's been eating my porridge," said Papa Bear.

Pretend!

Ask your child to pretend to be a bear walking in the woods. Have your child show you how a tiny baby bear would walk, how a medium-sized mother bear would walk, and how a great big father bear would walk. Then, ask your child to show you how each of these bears would eat porridge.

Sound It Out!

The word *bear* begins with the sound of the letter *B*. Brainstorm with your child other animal or insect names that begin with this sound. Some examples are *bat*, *beaver*, or *bumblebee*. Then, do the activity on page 153.

"Someone's been eating my porridge," said Mama Bear.

"Someone's been eating my porridge and has eaten it all up!" cried Baby Bear.

The three bears looked around the room.

"Someone's been sitting in my chair," said Papa Bear.

"Someone's been sitting in my chair," said Mama Bear.

"Someone's been sitting in my chair and has broken it to pieces!" cried Baby Bear.

Then, the three bears went into the bedroom.

"Someone's been sleeping on my bed," said Papa Bear.

"Someone's been sleeping on my bed," said Mama Bear.

"Someone's been sleeping on my bed and here she is!" cried Baby Bear.

Just then, Goldilocks woke up and saw the three bears. She jumped out of the bed and ran out the door.

Baby Bear hoped that Goldilocks would come back and play. But she never returned to the three bears' cottage in the woods.

B Is for Bear

Color the pictures whose names begin with the sound of the letter B.

The Three Billy Goats Gruff

Things to do next.

Add It On!

Add sound effects! As you read the story, have your child make trip-trapping noises each time a billy goat crosses the bridge. Also, let your child use a mean voice to help you say the troll's lines.

Be an Artist!

Give your child a sheet of paper and some crayons. Encourage your child to draw a picture of the troll from the story. To help your child get started, ask him or her to fill in the blanks. Trolls have _____ hair. Trolls have _____ noses. Trolls have _____ teeth.

Once upon a time, there were three Billy Goats Gruff, who were going to a grassy hillside to graze.

On the way, they had to cross a bridge, under which lived a mean troll.

First, the small Billy Goat Gruff started across the bridge.

Trip, trap, trip, trap.

"Who's that trip-trapping across my bridge?" roared the troll.

"It is I, the first Billy Goat Gruff. I would like to pass over your bridge."

"I'm very hungry," growled the troll. "So, I'm coming up to get you and eat you up."

"Oh, please don't eat me up!" said the first Billy Goat Gruff. "I'm not very big. Wait for my brother. He will be coming along soon, and he's much bigger!"

"Well, all right," said the troll, licking his lips. And he let the first Billy Goat Gruff pass over the bridge.

A while later, the medium-sized Billy Goat Gruff came along.

Trip, trap, trip, trap.

"Who's that trip-trapping across my bridge?" roared the troll.

"It is I, the second Billy Goat Gruff. I would like to pass over your bridge."

"I'm very hungry," growled the troll. "So, I'm coming up to get you and eat you up."

"Oh, please don't eat me up!" said the second Billy Goat Gruff. "I'm not very big. Wait for my brother. He will be along soon, and he's much bigger!"

"Well, all right," said the troll, licking his lips. And he let the second Billy Goat Gruff pass over the bridge.

A while later, along came the big Billy Goat Gruff.

TRIP, TRAP, TRIP, TRAP.

"Who's that trip-trapping across my bridge?" roared the troll.

Things to do next.

Brainstorm!

Brainstorm with your child to come up with names of big animals and little animals. Write down the names on a sheet of paper and see how many different animals you can come up with for each group. Then, do the activity on page 157.

Food Fun!

Make a grassy snack. Put some alfalfa sprouts and other kinds of lettuce in a bowl. Sprinkle the mixture with your child's favorite salad dressing. It might be messy, but encourage your child to try eating the salad without hands, using only his or her mouth just like a grazing goat!

Things to do next.

Pretend!

Have your child make a bridge out of blocks or empty plastic containers. Then, have your child use his or her fingers to act out the story. Use one hand to be the Billy Goats Gruff, walking across the bridge. Use the other hand to be the mean troll, who pops up and tries to grab the Billy Goat Gruffs.

Wiggle and Wriggle!

Designate an area of a hardwood or linoleum floor as an imaginary bridge. Have your child put on a pair of hard-heeled shoes and *trip, trap* across it. For the small Billy Goat, encourage your child to walk softly. For the largest Billy Goat, encourage your child to stomp heavily.

"It is I, the third Billy Goat Gruff. I would like to pass over your bridge."

"I'm very hungry," growled the troll. "So, I'm coming up to get you and eat you up."

"Well, come on then," said the third Billy Goat Gruff. "I have something for you."

The troll climbed onto the bridge and tried to grab the billy goat. But the third Billy Goat Gruff turned around and kicked the troll off the bridge with his strong back legs.

That was the last time the troll ever tried to stop anyone from crossing over the bridge.

And from that day on, the three Billy Goats Gruff grew fat from grazing on the grassy hill.

Super Sizes

Color the **big** shape in each box. Circle the **small** shape in each box.

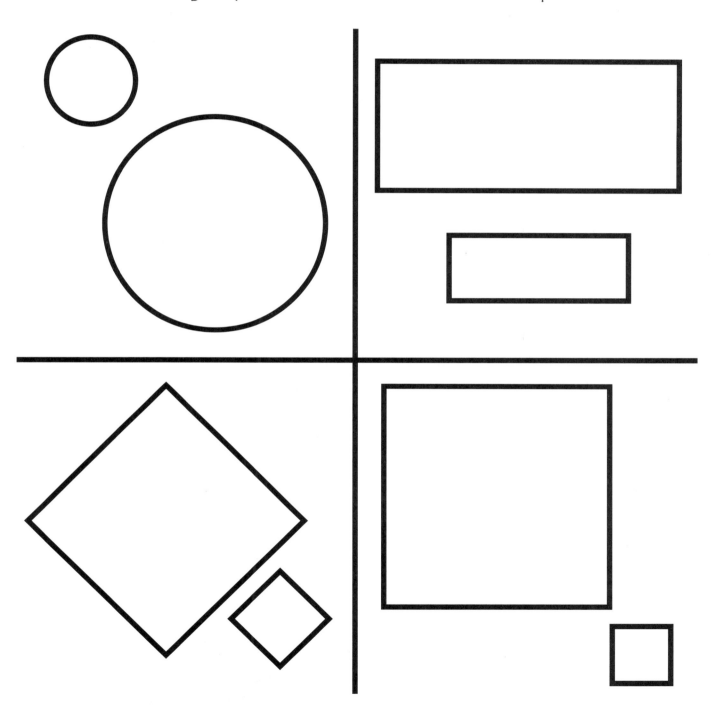

© 2006 School Specialty Publishing

Read, Sing, and Play Along! Lullaby Songs **157**

Things to do next.

Add It On!

Pretend that a set of blocks or empty plastic containers are bricks. Encourage your child to use them to build a house as high as possible and count them before they fall over!

Be an Artist!

Make a paper-plate pig. Give your child a paper plate and some crayons. Encourage your child to draw a pig's face on the plate, making sure to include the snout and ears. Complete the pig by taping a curly pipe-cleaner tail on the back of the plate!

Once upon a time, there were three little pigs, who lived at home with their mother.

One day, the three pigs decided to move out and build their own homes.

As they were walking down the road, they met a peddler with a cart full of straw.

The first little pig decided to buy some straw to build himself a house.

Next, the pigs met a peddler with a cart full of sticks.

The second little pig decided to buy some sticks to build himself a house.

Finally, the pigs met a peddler with a cart full of bricks.

The third little pig decided to buy some bricks to build a house for himself.

Then, the three pigs said goodbye to one another and went off to build their homes.

When the first little pig had finished building his house of straw, he heard a knock at the door.

It was a wolf, calling, "Little pig, little pig, let me come in."

"No, no!" cried the little pig. "Not by the hair of my chinny, chin, chin."

"Then, I'll huff, and I'll puff, and I'll blow your house in," said the wolf.

And he huffed, and he puffed, and he blew the house in.

The first little pig ran as fast as he could to the second pig's house, which was made of sticks.

Soon, they heard a knock at the door.

It was the wolf, and he said, "Little pigs, little pigs, let me come in."

"No, no!" they cried. "Not by the hair of our chinny, chin, chins."

"Then, I'll huff, and I'll puff, and I'll blow your house in," said the wolf.

Things to do next.

Can You Guess It?

Have your child close his or her eyes. Place a stick and then a piece of brick or stone in your child's hand. Can your child guess which material is which? Talk about the similarities and differences. Why would one material build a stronger house than the other?

Pretend!

Have your child pretend to be the big, bad wolf. On a table, place a variety of objects, such as a feather, cotton ball, book, and stone. Have your child try to blow each object by huffing and puffing like the wolf. Talk about which objects are easier to move.

Things to do next.

Sound It Out!

Brainstorm with your child a list of words that rhyme with *pig* (for example, *wig*, *dig*, and *big*).

Wiggle and Wriggle!

A pig's snout is very sensitive to touch, and many pigs use their snouts to dig up vegetable roots for food. Have your child pretend to be a pig. Encourage your child to crawl on all fours, oink, and use his or her snout to find imaginary food.

And he huffed, and he puffed, and he blew the house in.

The two little pigs ran as fast as they could to the third pig's house, which was made of bricks.

Soon, they heard a knock at the door.

It was the wolf, and he said, "Little pigs, little pigs, let me come in."

"No, no!" they cried. "Not by the hair of our chinny, chin, chins."

"Then, I'll huff, and I'll puff, and I'll blow your house in," said the wolf.

And he huffed, and he puffed, and he huffed, and he puffed, but he couldn't blow the house in.

Finally, he gave up and ran away, never to be seen again.

Home, Sweet Home

The three little pigs made their homes from different things.
Circle the homes that the three little pigs built.

The Wise Old Owl

Once upon a time, there were two little mice, who lived in a big old farmhouse.

The farmer didn't mind having the mice around, but the farmer's wife said they made too much of a mess. She wanted to get rid of them.

So, she went to the wise old owl and asked him what she could do.

"Simple," said the owl, "get a cat."

So, the farmer's wife brought home a cat. Soon, the mice were gone, but the cat often broke things when it jumped up on the furniture. This made the wife mad, so she went back to the wise old owl.

Things to do next.

Add It On!

Set out bowls of different kinds of O-shaped cereal and give your child resealable bags. Ask your child to count out ten pieces of one kind of cereal and put them in a bag. Then, ask your child to count out nine pieces of another kind to seal in another bag. Continue giving your child different number amounts to count.

Brainstorm!

The farmer's wife started with two mice in her house and ended up with two mice in her house. Was the owl really wise? Did he actually help the farmer's wife? What do you think the farmer's wife learned from the owl?

"Please, Mr. Owl, how can I get rid of the cat?"

"Simple," said the owl, "get a dog."

So, the woman got a dog and took it home. Soon, the cat was gone, but the woman wasn't happy. The dog barked too much and chewed up her slippers. Back went the woman to the owl.

"Mr. Owl, please tell me how I can get rid of the dog."

"Simple," said the owl, "get a tiger."

So, the farmer's wife bought a tiger and took it home. The dog left quickly, but much to her dismay, the woman watched the tiger run through her house, smashing everything in sight.

Back went the woman to the owl. "Mr. Owl, please tell me how I can get rid of a tiger."

Things to do next.

Be an Artist!

Illustrate this silly story! Use page 165 for your child's artwork.

Can You Guess It?

Have your child pick one of the animals from the story and pretend to be that animal. Try to guess which animal it is. Switch roles. Let your child try to guess which animal you are pretending to be!

Pretend to be owls.
Explain to your child
that owls stay very still,
often only moving
their eyes and heads.
Ask your child to look
at various objects
around the room,
moving only his or her
eyes and head to do so.
Next, ask your child to
pretend to be a mouse
and explain to you how
the two animals move
differently.

Sound It Out!

O is for *owl!* The word
owl begins with the
sound of the letter *O.*
Look through a
magazine with your
child. Point out pictures
of objects whose names
begin with the sound of
this letter.

"Simple," said the wise old owl, "get an
elephant."

Off the woman went. She bought an elephant
and took it home. When the tiger saw the elephant,
it left in a hurry. But the woman watched in horror
as the elephant broke windows and put holes
through walls. "Oh, no," cried the woman, "what
can I do?"

So, back she went to the owl. "Please, Mr. Owl,
tell me how I can get rid of an elephant."

"Simple," said the owl, "get two small mice!"

So, the woman went in search of two small mice
and took them home.

When the elephant saw the mice, it ran quickly
out of the house. And the farmer and his wife and
the two mice lived happily ever after in the big old
farmhouse.

Falling to Pieces!

Draw your favorite animal from the story in the box below. Draw over the entire puzzle. Cut the pieces apart, mix them up, and then put them back together again.

Left blank for cutting activity on previous page.

Alphabet Rhyme

A is for *apple*, B is for *ball*,
(*Pretend to eat apple. Bounce ball.*)

C is for *candy*, D is for *doll*.
(*Lick lips. Rock arms.*)

E is for *elephant*, F is for *frog*,
(*Make a trunk with one arm. Hop like a frog.*)

G is for *goose*, H is for *hog*.
(*Honk like a goose. Oink like a pig.*)

I is for *ice cream*, J is for *jam*,
(*Lick pretend ice-cream cone. Pretend to chew.*)

K is for *key*, L is for *lamb*.
(*Pretend to unlock door. Baa like a lamb.*)

M is for *monkey*, N is for *nail*,
(*Act like a monkey. Pretend to hammer a nail.*)

O is for *owl*, P is for *pail*.
(*Hoot like an owl. Pretend to carry a pail.*)

Q is for *queen*, R is for *rose*,
(*Use hands to make a pretend crown. Smell rose.*)

S is for *scissors*, T is for *toes*.
(*Use two fingers to make pretend scissors. Touch toes.*)

U is for *umbrella*, V is for *vase*,
(*Pretend to hold umbrella. Place vase on shelf.*)

W is for the *wind* that blows in my face.
(*Pretend to be swayed by the wind.*)

X is for *X-ray*, Y is for *you*,
(*Point to other person.*)

Z is for *zebra* in the zoo.
(*Prance like a zebra.*)

Things to do next.

Wiggle and Wriggle!

As you say each letter in the rhyme, see if your child can twist and move his or her body to make that letter!

Sound It Out!

Sing the alphabet song with your child! Then, have your child spell out his or her name and simple words using alphabet cereal or pasta.

Alphabet Wiggly Worm!

Write the missing letters on the wiggly worm to complete the alphabet!

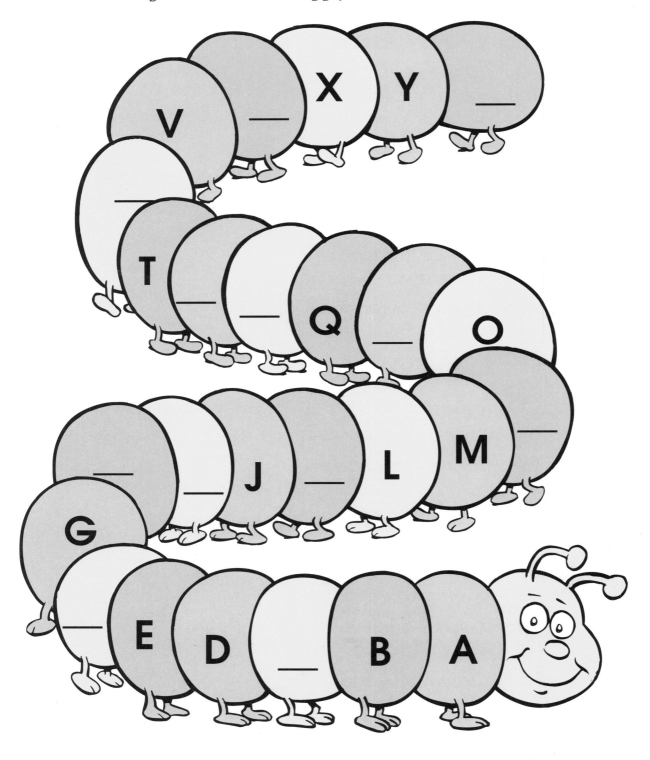

The Bear

Here is a cave,
(Make a fist.)
Inside is a bear.
(Put thumb inside fist.)
Now, he comes out
To get some fresh air.
(Pop out thumb.)

He stays out all summer
In sunshine and heat.
He hunts in the forest
For berries to eat.
(Move thumb in a circle.)

When snow starts to fall,
He hurries inside
His warm little cave,
And there he will hide.
(Put thumb back inside fist.)

Snow covers the cave
Like a fluffy white rug.
(Cover fist with other hand.)
Inside the bear sleeps
All cozy and snug.
(Pretend to be sleeping.)

Things to do next.

Pretend!

Bears hibernate, or sleep, all winter long. Have your child crawl on all fours, pretending to be a bear. Tell your child it's summer and encourage him or her to search for imaginary food. Then, tell your child it's winter time. Watch as your child exaggerates falling asleep!

Add It On!

Collect a large group of your child's teddy bears (or other stuffed animals). Let your child count the total number of bears. Sort the bears by category, such as color, size, those wearing bows, etc.

© 2006 School Specialty Publishing

Read, Sing, and Play Along! Lullaby Songs **169**

Things to do next.

Wiggle and Wriggle!

Encourage body awareness. Add additional verses to the rhyme, including different body parts. For example, try "Clap your hands, Touch your knee. Stamp your feet, Shout with glee." Make the verses as silly as possible!

Be an Artist!

Trace the outline of your child's body on a large sheet of paper or on the sidewalk with chalk. Help your child label the different parts of the body. Be as general or as specific as your child's skill level allows.

Clap Your Hands

(Do actions as rhyme indicates.)

Clap your hands,

Touch your toes.

Stamp your feet,

Wiggle your nose.

Clap your hands,

Touch your wrist.

Stamp your feet,

Make a fist.

Clap your hands,

Touch your hips.

Stamp your feet,

Smack your lips.

Clap your hands,

Touch your thighs.

Stamp your feet,

Blink your eyes.

Color Rhyme

(Do actions as rhyme indicates.)

If your clothes have any red,
Put your finger on your head.

If your clothes have any blue,
Put your finger on your shoe.

If your clothes have any green,
Wave your hand so that you're seen.

If your clothes have any yellow,
Smile like a happy fellow.

If your clothes have any brown,
Turn your smile into a frown.

If your clothes have any black,
Put your hands behind your back.

If your clothes have any white,
Stamp your feet with all your might.

Things to do next.

Brainstorm!

Look around the room. Give your child the name of a color and ask him or her to find an item in the room of that color. Continue until your child has found every color of the rainbow!

Be Silly!

Play a finger-twisting game! Use washable markers to draw a different colored dot on each finger of your child's left hand. Use the same colors to mark your child's right hand but change the order of the colors. Tell your child to put both red dots together, then both yellow dots together, etc.

Do You Suppose?

Do you suppose a giant,

Who is tall, tall, tall,

(Stretch high on tiptoe.)

Could ever be an elf,

Who is small, small, small?

(Crouch down.)

But the elf, who is tiny,

Will try, try, try,

(Stand and raise arms.)

To reach up to the giant,

Who is high, high, high.

(Stretch high on tiptoe.)

Things to do next.

Brainstorm!

The giant and the elf are opposites. Brainstorm with your child other pairs of opposites that are big and small (for example, an ant and an elephant or a cup of water and a swimming pool).

Be an Artist!

Give your child a sheet of paper and some crayons. Have your child draw a picture of the tall, tall giant and the small, small elf! Call attention to the lengths of their legs and arms.

Draw for Me

Draw a circle
round as can be.

(Draw circle in the air.)

Draw a circle
Just for me.

(Point to self.)

Draw a square
Shaped like a door.

(Draw square in the air.)

Draw a square
With corners four.

(Hold up four fingers.)

Draw a triangle
With corners three.

(Draw a triangle in the air.)

Draw a triangle
Just for me!

(Point to self.)

Things to do next.

Wiggle and Wriggle!

Say the rhyme again. Have your child try to make each shape by twisting his or her body into different positions!

Add It On!

Find items around the house that represent different shapes. For example, you might use a cereal box for a rectangle, a ball for a circle, and a cracker for a square. Give your child the name of a shape and have your child pick up the item in the pile that matches it. Then, do the shape activity on page 174!

Name That Shape!

Draw a line to match the shapes.

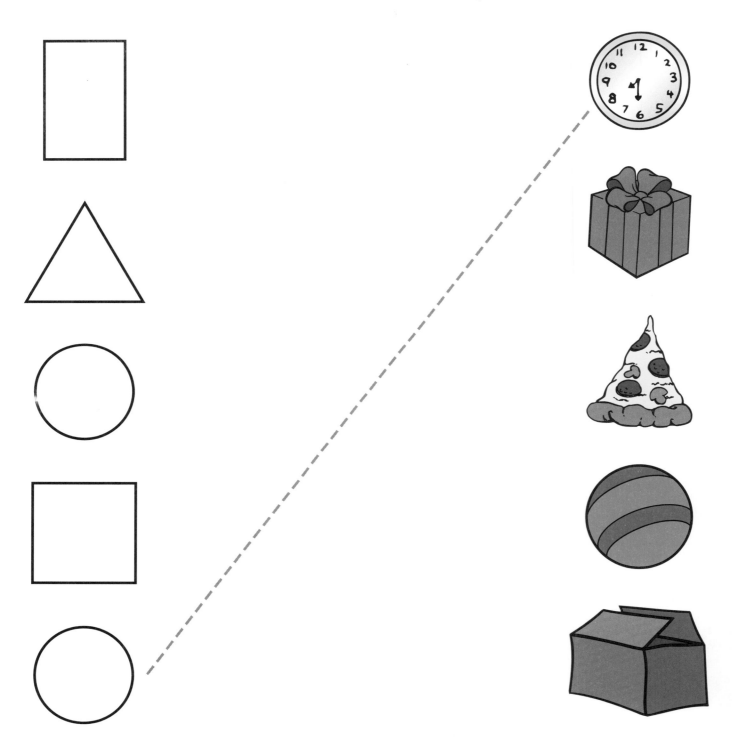

Read, Sing, and Play Along! Lullaby Songs

The Eeensy, Weensy Spider

The eensy, weensy spider
Went up the water spout.

(Crawl fingers up high.)

Down came the rain
And washed the spider out.

(Drop fingers quickly.)

Out came the sun
And dried up all the rain.

(Form a circle with arms.)

And the eensy, weensy spider
Went up the spout again.

(Crawl fingers back up high.)

Things to do next.

Pretend!

Pretend to be a spider! Have your child crawl on all fours and scurry across the floor.

Be an Artist!

Make a spider web. Give your child a sheet of paper and some black yarn. Use glue to make the pattern of a spider's web. Have your child attach the yarn to the gluey web. After it dries, draw a spider!

Things to do next.

Add It On!

Trace your child's hands on a sheet of paper. Ask your child to identify the thumb, pointer finger, middle finger, etc. Use the fingers to count to ten with your child!

Can You Guess It?

Put both of your hands behind your back. Bring one hand in front of you and hold up a certain number of fingers. Quickly, move the hand behind your back again. See if your child can count the number of fingers you held up!

Fee, fie, fo, fum.

See my finger,

(Hold up pointer finger.)

See my thumb.

(Hold up thumb.)

Fee, fie, fo, fum,

Finger's gone,

(Bend pointer finger down.)

So is thumb!

(Hide thumb in fist.)

Five Little Farmers

Five little farmers
Woke up with the sun.
(Hold up five fingers.)
It was early morning.
There were chores to be done.
(Wiggle fingers.)

The first little farmer
Went to milk the cow.
(Point to thumb.)
The second little farmer
Decided he would plow.
(Point to index finger.)

The third little farmer
Fed the hungry hens.
(Point to middle finger.)
The fourth little farmer
Mended broken pens.
(Point to ring finger.)

The fifth little farmer
Took his vegetables to town.
(Point to little finger.)
Baskets filled with cabbages
And sweet potatoes brown.

Things to do next.

Sound It Out!

The word *farmer* begins with the sound of the letter *F*. So do the words *five* and *finger*. Ask your child to identify other familiar words that begin with this sound.

Brainstorm!

Lots of different animals live on a farm. Brainstorm with your child a list of all these animals. Talk about the different noises these animals make, the kinds of food they eat, and the work they do on a farm.

Five Purple Polka Dots

Things to do next.

Add It On!

Cut out circle shapes from a purple sheet of paper. Then, cut square shapes from a different color of paper. Arrange the shapes in a simple pattern (for example, circle—circle—square—circle—circle—square). Have your child continue the pattern by adding the shapes that come next. Try different patterns.

Be an Artist!

Give your child a sheet of paper and a purple crayon or marker. Encourage your child to draw five purple polka dots. Add features, such as a face, hair, legs, and arms. Give each polka dot a name but make sure it starts with the sound of the letter *P!*

Five purple polka dots sitting on the floor,
(Hold up five fingers.)
One crawled away, and then, there were four.
(Bend down thumb.)

Four purple polka dots got on their knees,
One tipped over, and then, there were three.
(Bend down pointer finger.)

Three purple polka dots stood on one shoe,
One fell down, and then, there were two.
(Bend down middle finger.)

Two purple polka dots started to run,
One stopped quickly, and then, there was one.
(Bend down ring finger.)

One purple polka dot rolled out the door,
When it disappeared, there were no more!
(Bend down little finger.)

Five Shiny Marbles

Five shiny marbles lying on the floor,
(Hold up five fingers.)
One shoots away, and that leaves four.
(Bend down thumb.)

Four shiny marbles I can plainly see,
One rolls off, and that leaves three.
(Bend down pointer finger.)

Three shiny marbles, now just a few,
One spins away, and that leaves two.
(Bend down middle finger.)

Two shiny marbles sparkling in the sun,
One wanders off, and that leaves one.
(Bend down ring finger.)

One shiny marble looking for some fun,
Goes off to find the others, and that leaves none!
(Bend down little finger.)

Things to do next.

Wiggle and Wriggle!

Pretend to be a marble. Lay down a blanket or soft mat. Help your child roll over and over—just like a marble!

Food Fun!

As a special treat, serve your child a round snack, such as chocolate-covered malted milk balls. For a healthy option, serve grapes or blueberries.

Things to do next.

Add It On!

Make a sock doll. Stuff a clean sock with fabric scraps or cotton balls. Tie pieces of yarn around the stuffed sock to make a head, body, and legs. Let your child add a face with markers. Add yarn for hair.

Wiggle and Wriggle!

Play hide-and-seek. Have your child grab a couple of his or her favorite dolls or stuffed animals. Then, while your child isn't looking, hide them around the room. See if your child can find all these friends!

Floppy Rag Doll

(Do actions as rhyme indicates.)

Flop your arms, flop your feet,
Let your hands go free.

Flop your head, flop your legs,
Fall down to your knees.

Flowers in My Garden

One purple flower in my garden grew,
(Hold up one finger.)
Up popped another, and that made two.
(Hold up two fingers.)

Two purple flowers were all that I could see,
But then I found another, and that made three.
(Hold up three fingers.)

Three purple flowers—if I could find one more,
I'd put them in a tiny vase, and that would make four.
(Hold up four fingers.)

Four purple flowers, sure as we're alive,
Oh, here's another one, now that makes five!
(Hold up five fingers.)

Things to do next.

Be an Artist!

Look through old magazines with your child and point out different pictures of flowers. Tear out the pictures and help your child glue them to a sheet of paper to make a beautiful flower garden!

Wiggle and Wriggle!

Go outside for a nature walk. If the season permits, pick wild flowers with your child. Or go to a florist shop. Talk about the color of the flowers, their smell, and their shape. Then, do the flower activity on page 182.

Favorite Flowers!

Draw five of your favorite flowers in the flower box.

Give It a Shake

Tune: The Hokey Pokey

(Do actions as rhyme indicates.)

You put one finger up,

You put one finger down,

You put one finger up,

And you shake it all around.

You give it a shakey-shakey,

And you turn it all about.

That's how you learn to count!

Wiggle and Wriggle!

Do the traditional hokey pokey with your child! Include body parts such as the arms, legs, and head.

Be an Artist!

Make a shaker. Find an old plastic container, such as a milk jug or a soda pop container. Fill the container with seeds, beans, bells, washers, or gravel. Let your child decorate the container and shake it as you sing the song again.

Hickory, Dickory, Dock

Things to do next.

Wiggle and Wriggle!

Play a clock game with your child. Tell your child a time and let him or her loudly "bong" out the correct number of strikes on the clock for this time. For example, if you say "11 o'clock," your child should make a bonging sound 11 times. Then, do the clock activity on page 185!

Be Silly!

Create new nonsense verses for this rhyme. For example, "The clock struck two. The mouse didn't know what to do." Try thinking of verses that include numbers 2 through 10.

Hickory, dickory, dock.

The mouse ran up the clock.

(Run fingers up arm.)

The clock struck one.

(Clap hands once.)

The mouse ran down.

(Run fingers down arm.)

Hickory, dickory, dock.

Tick-Tock, Tick-Tock

Trace the numbers 1 through 12 on the clock.

 What time is on the clock? _____

I Can Count

One, two, three, four.

(Count four fingers on one hand.)

I can count even more.

Five, six, seven, eight.

(Count four fingers on other hand.)

My little fingers stand up straight.

Nine and ten

(Make fists and hold up thumbs.)

Are my two thumb men.

Things to do next.

Add It On!

Have your child wiggle all ten fingers in the air. Then, encourage your child to count to ten using his or her fingers. Say the rhyme again. This time, have your child count to ten using his or her toes!

Add It On!

Number ten index cards from 1 to 10 with numbers and corresponding sets of dots. Mix up the cards. Have your child count the dots on each card and arrange them in numerical order. When the cards are in the correct order, let your child countdown while pointing to each card. After number 1, yell, "Blast off!"

I Look in the Mirror

I look in the mirror,

(Pretend to look in mirror.)

And what do I see?

I see a happy face,

(Smile.)

Smiling at me.

I look in the mirror,

(Pretend to look in mirror.)

And what do I see?

I see a sad face,

(Frown.)

Frowning at me.

Things to do next.

Can You Guess It?

Make a face and see if your child can guess which emotion you're trying to imitate. For example, make a grumpy, sleepy, or surprised face.

Be an Artist!

Give your child a blank doll shape cut out of paper. Look in the mirror with your child and talk about his or her hair color, eye color, and freckles. Have your child make the paper doll look just like himself or herself. Then, do the face activity on page 188!

What's Missing?

Draw the missing parts on each face below.

Now, draw your own face!

I'm a Choo-Choo Train

I'm a choo-choo train,

(Bend arms at sides.)

Chugging down the track.

(Rotate arms in rhythm.)

First, I go forward.

(Rotate arms forward.)

Then, I go back.

(Rotate arms back.)

Now, my bell is ringing,

(Pretend to pull bell cord.)

Hear my whistle blow.

(Toot into a closed fist.)

What a lot of noise I make,

(Place hands over ears.)

Everywhere I go!

(Stretch arms out at sides.)

Things to do next.

Pretend!

Tell your child you are going on an imaginary train ride. Let your child be the conductor. Put your hands on your child's shoulders and let him or her lead you around the house!

Food Fun!

Have a *T* party. For a snack, serve your child foods and beverages that start with the letter *T*. Include things like tuna fish sandwiches, taco chips, or toast. Serve tea or tomato juice.

I'm a Little Monkey

I'm a little monkey. Watch me play,

(Hop around near floor.)

Munching on bananas every day.

(Pretend to eat banana.)

I have monkey friends, who play with me.

(Point to other.)

See us climb right up the tree!

(Make climbing movements.)

Things to do next.

Food Fun!

Serve your child a snack fit for a monkey—bananas! Add peanut butter to the slices for a tasty variation.

Wiggle and Wriggle!

Print the letter M on five or six index cards and print other letters on several more cards. Show the cards to your child. Whenever your child sees an M, have him or her jump up and down and act like a monkey.

I'm the Sun

I'm the sun, so big and bright.

(Make circle with arms and hold it over head.)

I shine on earth and make it light.

(Stretch arms at sides.)

I keep you warm.

(Rub upper arms.)

I help you grow.

(Stand on tiptoe and stretch arms to sky.)

I let you see your shadow.

(Cup hands around eyes.)

Things to do next.

Brainstorm!

Talk with your child about the importance of the sun. What good things does the sun do for us? For example, it provides heat, energy, and helps plants to grow.

Be an Artist!

Make sun visors. Cut a paper plate in half. Let your child decorate one half of the plate with crayons, markers, and stickers. Use a hole punch to punch two holes in the plate, one on each end of the straight edge. Add yarn as a tie and wear the visor outside in the sun!

Things to do next.

Add It On!

Help your child count all of the pockets on his or her own clothing. Then, have your child count how many pockets are on your clothing. What is the total?

Add It On!

Number ten envelopes from 1 to 10 to make pockets. Give your child a handful of buttons, dried beans, or paperclips. Encourage your child to count the correct number of items for each pocket and put them inside.

The things in my pockets are lots of fun.
(Hold up five fingers.)
I will show you one by one.

In my first pocket is a frog.
(Point to thumb.)
I found him sitting on a log.

In my second pocket is a car.
(Point to index finger.)
It can race off very far.

In my third pocket is a ball.
(Point to middle finger.)
I can bounce it on a wall.

In my fourth pocket is a bunny.
(Point to ring finger.)
It twitches its nose and looks so funny.

In my fifth pocket is a dog.
(Point to little finger.)
He's a friend of my little frog.
(Touch little finger to thumb.)

Jack-in-the-Box

Jack-in-the-box,

You sit so still.

(Make fist with thumb inside.)

Won't you come out?

Yes, I will!

(Pop out thumb.)

Wiggle and Wriggle!

Repeat the rhyme. This time, have your child crouch down near the floor. At the end of the poem, have your child jump up and yell, "Yes, I will!"

Add It On!

Put together a deck of playing cards that includes the jacks from several decks. Have your child sort through the cards and find all of the jacks. Count them!

Things to do next.

Wiggle and Wriggle!

Let your child jump up and down as you repeat the rhyme. Then, try jumping rope or doing jumping jacks!

Sound It Out!

The word *jump* begins with the sound of the letter *J*. Help your child cut the shape of a *J* out of construction paper. Then, have your child tell you the names of items whose names begin with this sound!

Kids on the Bed

Five little kids were jumping on the bed,
(Hold up five fingers.)
One fell down and bumped his head.
(Bend down thumb.)
He fell off and rolled out the door.
Kids on the bed? Now, there are four.

Four little kids were jumping on the bed,
One fell down and bumped her head.
(Bend down pointer finger.)
She fell off and bruised her knee.
Kids on the bed? Now, there are three.

Three little kids were jumping on the bed,
One fell down and bumped his head.
(Bend down middle finger.)
He fell off. He's black and blue.
Kids on the bed? Now, there are two.

Two little kids were jumping on the bed,
One fell down and bumped her head.
(Bend down ring finger.)
She fell off, no more fun.
Kids on the bed? Now, there is one.

One little kid was jumping on the bed,
This is what his mother said,
"No more jumping, turn out the light.
Now, it's time to say goodnight!"
(Bend down little finger and say, "Goodnight!")

Kite Friends

One little kite in the sky so blue,
Along came another, then there were two.
(Hold up one finger, then two fingers.)

Two little kites flying high above me,
Along came another, then there were three.
(Hold up three fingers.)

Three little kites, just watch how they soar,
Along came another, then there were four.
(Hold up four fingers.)

Four little kites, so high and alive,
Along came another, then there were five.
(Hold up five fingers.)

Five little kites dancing 'cross the sky,
What a sight to see, way up so high!
(Dance all five fingers in air.)

Things to do next.

Wiggle and Wriggle!

If possible, go outside on a windy day and fly a kite! Or have your child pretend to be a kite while you pretend to be the kite flyer. Hold on to the imaginary string as your child swirls, swoops, and soars around the room.

Be an Artist!

Cut a diamond out of construction paper. Let your child decorate the diamond with crayons and markers. Add a piece of yarn as a tail and hang it on the wall or refrigerator.

Little Cow

Things to do next.

Wiggle and Wriggle!

Talk with your child about cows and how they give us much of the milk we need. Then, let your child pretend to milk a cow!

Be an Artist!

Give your child a sheet of paper and some crayons. Have your child draw a picture of a cow. Then, go outside to a grassy area and pick blades of grass. Help your child glue the grass to the bottom of the picture.

This little cow eats grass.

(Point to thumb.)

This little cow eats hay.

(Point to index finger.)

This little cow drinks water.

(Point to middle finger.)

This little cow runs away.

(Point to ring finger.)

And this little cow does nothing at all

(Point to little finger.)

But chew her cud all day.

One Potato, Two Potato

One potato, two potato,

(Count on fingers.)

Three potato, four,

Five potato, six potato,

Seven potato, more.

Eight potato, nine potato,

Here is ten.

Now, let's count

All over again!

Things to do next.

Wiggle and Wriggle!

Have your child hop on one foot for the first line of the poem. Then, have your child switch legs for the second line. Continue hopping on one foot and then the other to the beat of the rhyme.

Be an Artist!

Try potato printing. Carefully cut a potato in half. Then, press a simple-shaped cookie cutter into the flat surface of a halved potato. Remove the excess potato and help your child dip the potato into some paint. Press the potato onto a piece of paper. Presto: a potato print!

© 2006 School Specialty Publishing

Read, Sing, and Play Along! Lullaby Songs **197**

Things to do next.

Brainstorm!

Ask your child to name all of the colors in the rainbow. Then, brainstorm several items for each color your child names. Try using different themes. For example, think of rainbow-colored foods or flowers.

Add It On!

Make a rainbow! On a sunny day, go outside and stand with your back facing the sun. Turn on a water hose and look in the water spray to find the rainbow.

Rainbow Rhyme

Tune: Twinkle, Twinkle, Little Star

When the rain falls from the sky,
(Flutter fingers downward.)
Don't forget to look up high.
(Cup hand above eyes and look up.)
If the sun is shining there,
(Make a circle with arms above head.)
You may find a rainbow fair.
(Sweep arms in an arc above head.)
Red, orange, yellow, green, and blue,
And you'll see there's purple too.

Rainy Day

Rain on the green grass,

(Flutter fingers downward.)

And rain on the tree.

(Flutter fingers up over head.)

Rain on the housetop,

(Make upside-down V with hands and arms.)

But not on me.

(Circle arms over head to make umbrella.)

Things to do next.

Wiggle and Wriggle!

Place several pillows or mats on the floor. Tell your child these are imaginary rain puddles. Have your child practice jumping over and in the puddles!

Be an Artist!

Make rain! Boil some water in a pan or kettle until steam forms above it. Then, fill a pie pan with ice cubes and hold it above the steam. Show your child how water droplets form when steam comes in contact with the cool air from the pie pan. It's just like rain!

Shadows

Shadows dance upon the wall,

Shadows big and very tall.

(Raise arms high.)

Shadows follow me around,

Shadows never make a sound.

(Put finger to lips and shake head.)

Shadows down beside my feet,

Shadows everywhere I peek.

(Point to floor, then peek around.)

Things to do next.

Wiggle and Wriggle!

Find a bright light to shine on you and cast your shadow on the wall. Show your child how your shadow can move. Encourage your child to make his or her own shadow dance, twirl, wave, and even fall down!

Be an Artist!

Give your child a sheet of white paper and crayons. Go outside and hold the paper directly behind a leaf, a flower, or some grass so that the object's shadow falls on the paper. Then, trace the shadow to create a shadow creation!

Silly Shadows

Look at the shadow shapes in the first column.
Draw a line from the shadow to the picture it matches.

© 2006 School Specialty Publishing

Read, Sing, and Play Along! Lullaby Songs **201**

Six Buzzing Bumblebees

Sound It Out!

Play a game with your child. Start by saying, "B, B, what begins with B?" Choose something in the room that begins with the sound of this letter. Give your child five tries to guess the object you're thinking of. Then, let your child pick a *B* object while you guess.

Food Fun!

Talk to your child about how bees produce honey. Then, let your child dip carrot sticks, apple slices, or orange segments into some honey for a sweet bee snack!

Six Buzzing Bumblebees

Six buzzing bumblebees flying 'round the hive,
(Hold up six fingers.)
One buzzes off, and that leaves five.
(Hold up five fingers.)

Five buzzing bumblebees flying near my door,
One buzzes off, and that leaves four.
(Bend down thumb.)

Four buzzing bumblebees flying 'round my tree,
One buzzes off, and that leaves three.
(Bend down pointer finger.)

Three buzzing bumblebees in the sky so blue,
One buzzes off, and that leaves two.
(Bend down middle finger.)

Two buzzing bumblebees flying by the sun,
One buzzes off, and that leaves one.
(Bend down ring finger.)

One buzzing bumblebee looking for some fun,
It buzzes off, and that leaves none.
(Bend down little finger.)

Teddy Bear, Teddy Bear, Turn Around

(Do actions as rhyme indicates.)

Teddy bear, teddy bear, turn around.

Teddy bear, teddy bear, touch the ground.

Teddy bear, teddy bear, reach up high.

Teddy bear, teddy bear, touch the sky.

Teddy bear, teddy bear, bend down low.

Teddy bear, teddy bear, touch your toe.

Things to do next.

Be Silly!

Repeat the rhyme, but this time, add a different character. For example, say, "Purple hippo, purple hippo, turn around." Make up as many nonsense verses as possible.

Be an Artist!

Cut a teddy bear shape out of cardboard or posterboard. Punch holes around the edges with a hole punch. Then, let your child lace a piece of colorful yarn through the holes.

Things to do next.

Add It On!

Recite the nursery rhyme *Jack, Be Nimble!* with your child. Place an unlit candle on the floor and have your child jump over it! Then, do the activity on page 205.

Add It On!

Collect as many different sizes and shapes of candles as you can. Encourage your child to line them up from shortest to tallest or from smallest to largest. Arrange the candles in groups of two. Then, use the candles to practice counting by twos with your child.

Ten Little Candles

Ten little candles standing on a cake.
(Hold up ten fingers.)
Whh! Whh! Now, there are eight.
(Blow twice and bend down two fingers.)

Eight little candles in candle sticks.
Whh! Whh! Now, there are six.
(Blow twice and bend down two fingers.)

Six little candles, not one more.
Whh! Whh! Now, there are four.
(Blow twice and bend down two fingers.)

Four little candles, yellow and blue.
Whh! Whh! Now, there are two.
(Blow twice and bend down two fingers.)

Two little candles, one plus one.
Whh! Whh! Now, there are none.
(Blow twice and bend down two fingers.)

Counting Candles!

Color the spaces:

1 = brown   3 = yellow
2 = green   4 = purple

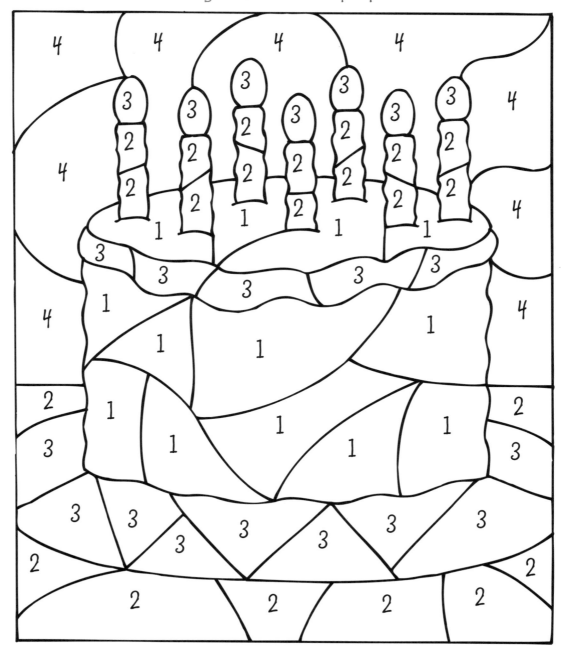

Two Little Feet Go Tap

Two little feet go tap, tap, tap,
(Tap feet.)
Two little hands go clap, clap, clap,
(Clap hands.)
A quick little leap up from my chair,
(Stand up quickly.)
Two little arms reach high in the air.
(Stretch arms high.)

Two little feet go jump, jump, jump,
(Jump.)
Two little fists go thump, thump, thump,
(Pound fists.)
One little body goes round and round,
(Twirl around.)
And one little child sits quietly down.
(Sit down.)

Things to do next.

Can You Guess It?

Look through magazines or books with your child for pictures of all kinds of feet. Count the total number of feet on the different objects you see.

Be an Artist!

Make a foot butterfly! Trace your child's feet on a sheet of paper. Use the feet as the butterfly's wings. Add a butterfly body between each foot and antennae. Then, encourage your child to color the beautiful butterfly!

Wake Up, Little Fingers

Wake up, little fingers, the morning has come.

(Slowly open fists.)

Now, hold them up, every finger and thumb.

(Hold fingers up straight.)

Come jump out of bed, see how tall you can stand.

(Raise outstretched hands.)

Oh, my, you are such a wide-awake band.

(Clap hands once.)

You have all washed your faces, and you look so neat.

(Rub hands together, then fold them.)

Now, come to the table and let us all eat.

(Pretend to eat.)

Now, all you fingers run out to play,

(Wiggle and dance fingers.)

And have a good time on this beautiful day!

(Smile!)

Things to do next.

Wiggle and Wriggle!

Have your child examine his or her hands. Experiment with different ways of moving his or her hands, fingers, and wrists. Can your child snap? How far apart can your child spread his or her fingers? Can your child cross his or her fingers?

Be an Artist!

Give your child a large sheet of paper and some finger paint. Then, turn on music and have your child paint to the beat. Encourage your child to move his or her fingers to the rhythm and tempo of the music.

Wee Willie Winkie

Things to do next.

Be Silly!

Have your child run through the house, knocking on each door and saying "Now, it's eight o'clock!"

Food Fun!

Fix some *W* snacks! Let your child feast on watermelon, walnuts, wheat crackers, or candy worms.

Wee Willie Winkie runs through the town,

(Run in place.)

Upstairs and downstairs in his nightgown,

Rapping at the window, crying through the lock,

(Pretend to knock, then hold fist up to mouth.)

"Are the children in their beds?

For now it's eight o'clock!"

When a Yellow Duck

When a yellow duck walks down the street,

(Hold up hand.)

Quack! goes his bill.

(Open and close thumb and index finger.)

Waddle! go his feet.

(Waddle hand back and forth.)

He comes to a puddle and with a bound,

(Form circle with opposite arm.)

In goes the yellow duck and swims around.

(Jump hand into circle and move it around.)

Things to do next.

Pretend!

Pretend to be yellow ducks. Waddle around the room and quack a hello greeting when you pass by each other. Swim in an imaginary pond and look for imaginary plants and seeds to eat.

Be an Artist!

Cut out a duck shape from paper. Give your child glue and let him or her glue feathers (available at craft stores) to the shape. Glue a craft stick to the back and let your child use the duck to act out the rhyme.

Things to do next.

Add It On!

Now say the additional verses:

1. Where is pointer?
2. Where is tall man?
3. Where is ring man?
4. Where is small man?

Wiggle and Wriggle!

Talk with your child about how our thumbs help us hold things firmly. Have your child try to pick up things without using his or her thumbs. Let your child try to eat a snack without using his or her thumbs.

Where Is Thumbkin?

Where is thumbkin? Where is thumbkin?

(Put hands behind back.)

Here I am!

(Bring one thumb forward.)

Here I am!

(Bring other thumb forward.)

How are you today, sir?

(Wiggle one thumb.)

Very well, I thank you.

(Wiggle other thumb.)

Run away. Run away.

(Put hands behind back.)

Who Will Feed the Baby?

Who will feed the baby?
(Make feeding motions.)
Who will go to the store?
(Make fingers run.)
Who will cook the dinner?
(Make stirring motions.)
Who will clean the floor?
(Make scrubbing motions.)

Who will wash the clothes?
(Pretend to wash clothes.)
Who will cut the grass?
(Pretend to mow lawn.)
Who will wash the car?
(Pretend to wash car.)
Who will get the gas?
(Pretend to steer car.)

If everybody helps,
The work will soon be done.
Then, there will be more time
For having lots of fun!
(Raise arms and shout "Hurray!")

Things to do next.

Brainstorm!

Brainstorm with your child a list of chores that need to be done in your house every week. Designate two or three chores for your child to do for one week. Make a chart. Every time your child completes the chore, give him or her a star! Switch chores for the next week.

Can You Guess It?

Act out one of the chores from the rhyme. Can your child guess which action you are pretending to do? Switch roles. Let your child act out a chore and you try to guess.

© 2006 School Specialty Publishing

Read, Sing, and Play Along! Lullaby Songs **211**

Wiggle Your Toes

(Do actions as rhyme indicates.)

Wiggle your toes, wiggle your toes,

Wiggle them up and down.

Wiggle them fast, wiggle them slow,

Wiggle them all around.

Things to do next.

Add It On!

Now say the additional verses:

1. Wave your hands.
2. Stamp your feet.
3. Blink your eyes.

Wiggle and Wriggle!

Place a large sheet of paper on the ground. Trace your child's feet in random spots all over the paper. Color in the footprints. Then, have your child step onto the paper and match his or her feet in two footprints. When you say "Switch," have your child jump onto two more footprints.

Sheet Music

All Through the Night

Words and Music
Traditional
Arranged by
Hal Wright

Sleep my love, and peace at-tend thee, all through the night.
Ang - els watch-ing ev - er 'round thee, all through the night.

Guard - ian ang - els God will lend thee, all through the night.
In thy slumb - ers close sur-round thee, all through the night.

Armenian Lullaby

Words and Music
Traditional
Arranged by
Hal Wright

Sleep, my lit - tle one, my ____ loved one,
as I rock and sing, as the bright ____

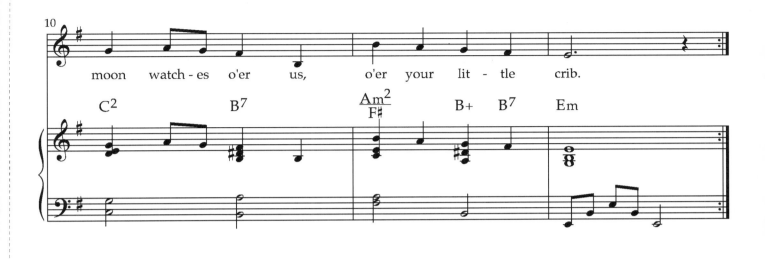

moon watch - es o'er us, o'er your lit - tle crib.

Baa, Baa, Black Sheep

Words and Music
Traditional
Arranged by
Hal Wright

one   for the lit - tle boy who   lives   down the lane.

Baloo Baleerie

Words and Music
Traditional
Arranged by
Hal Wright

Brahms' Lullaby

Words by
Karl Simrock
Music by
Johannes Brahms
Arranged by
Hal Wright

= 90 Sweetly
C2
Am9
Am/F♯
4
Lul - la - by and good night, with
G13
C2
Am9
7
ro - ses de - light, with lil - ies be -
Am/F♯
F/G
G
Dm7

© 2006 Twin Sisters IP, LLC. All Rights Reserved.

Read, Sing, and Play Along! Lullaby Songs **223**

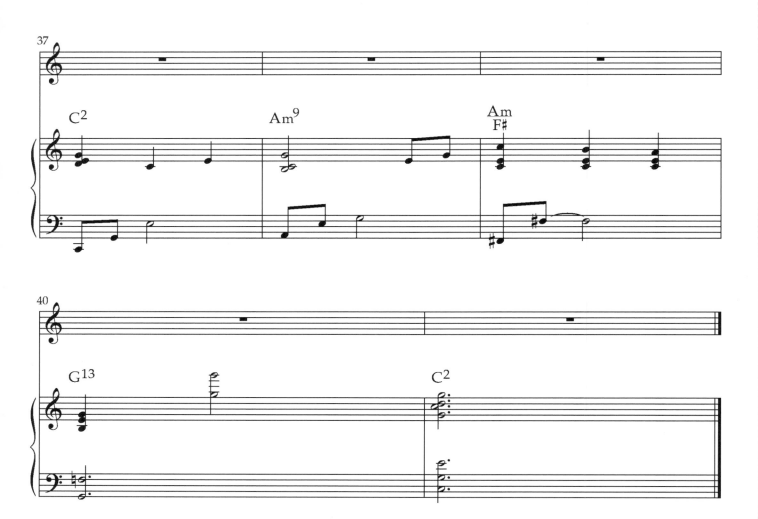

Bye, Baby Bunting

Words and Music
Traditional
Arranged by
Hal Wright

rab - bit skin to wrap his ba - by bunt - ing in.

Dance to Your Daddy

Words and Music
Traditional
Arranged by
Hal Wright

Georgie Porgie

Words and Music
Traditional
Arranged by
Hal Wright

Geor - gie Por - gie, pud-din' and pie, kissed the girls and made them cry.

When the boys came out to play, Geor - gie Por - gie ran a-way.

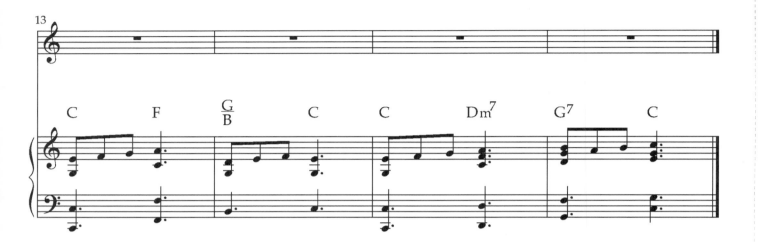

Go to Sleep,
My Sweet Little Brother

Words and Music
Traditional
Arranged by
Hal Wright

© 2006 Twin Sisters IP, LLC. All Rights Reserved.

Read, Sing, and Play Along! Lullaby Songs   **233**

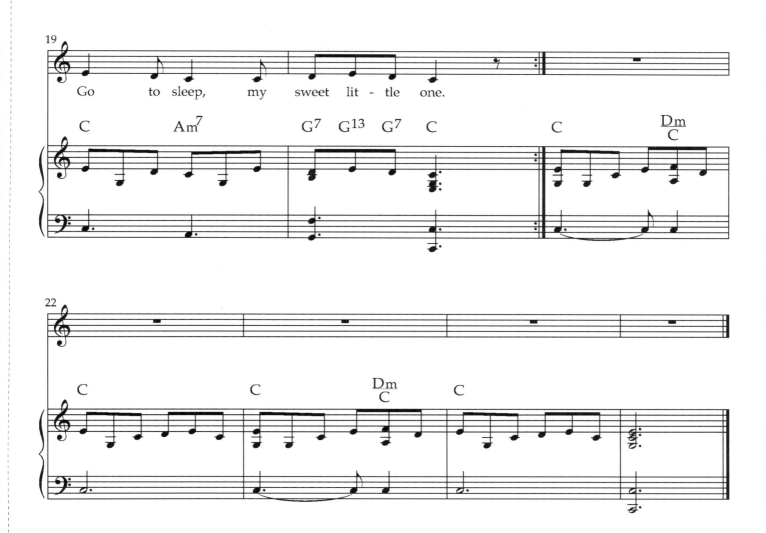

Go to sleep, my sweet lit - tle one.

© 2006 Twin Sisters IP, LLC. All Rights Reserved.

Read, Sing, and Play Along! Lullaby Songs   **235**

Go to Sleep

Words and Music
Traditional
Arranged by
Hal Wright

here by my side. I will not ev-er, no,

G7   G9   Am7 $\frac{C\triangle^7}{E}$ $\frac{G}{F}$ F Em

nev-er let you go. Go to sleep,

Dm7   G9   C   C△7 $\frac{F}{G}$ G7 C   C△7

go to sleep, sleep, sleep. Go to sleep,

Dm7   Gsus7   G $\frac{G^{13}}{F}$ $\frac{C^2}{E}$

Golden Slumbers

Words and Music
Traditional
Arranged by
Hal Wright

Hickety Pickety, My Black Hen

Words and Music
Traditional
Arranged by
Hal Wright

Hick - et - y Pick - et - y, my black hen.

Hickory Dickory Dock

Words and Music
Traditional
Arranged by
Hal Wright

Hush, Little Baby

Words and Music
Traditional
Arranged by
Hal Wright

And if that billy goat won't pull, Mama's going to buy you a cart and bull.

And if that cart and bull turn over, Mama's going to buy you a dog named Rover.

And if that dog named Rover won't bark, Mama's going to buy you a horse and cart.

And if that horse and cart fall down, you'll still be the sweetest little baby in town.

Jack and Jill

Words and Music by
J. W. Elliot
Arranged by
Hal Wright

Jack and Jill went up the hill to fetch a pail of wa - ter.
Up Jack got and home did trot as fast as he could ca - per.

Jack fell down and broke his crown, and Jill___ came tum - bling af - ter.
Went to bed to mend his head with vin - e - gar and brown pa - per.

Kum Ba Yah

Words and Music
Traditional
Arranged by
Hal Wright

Kum ba yah, my Lord,_____ kum ba yah._____

Lord, _____ kum ba yah. _____

Little Boy Blue

Words and Music
Traditional
Arranged by
Hal Wright

un - der the hay - stack fast a - sleep.

London Bridge

Words and Music
Traditional
Arranged by
Hal Wright

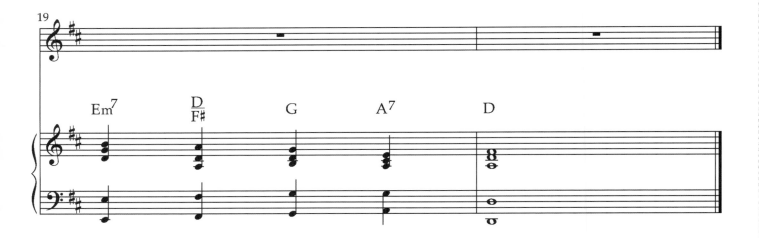

Other optional verses:

Gold and silver, I have none, I have none, I have none.
Gold and silver, I have none, my fair lady.

Build it up with needles and pins, needles and pins, needles and pins.
Build it up with needles and pins, my fair lady.

Pins and needles bend and break, bend and break, bend and break.
Pins and needles bend and break, my fair lady.

Build it up with wood and clay, wood and clay, wood and clay.
Build it up with wood and clay, my fair lady.

Wood and clay will wash away, wash away, wash away.
Wood and clay will wash away, my fair lady.

Build it up with stone so strong, stone so strong, stone so strong.
Build it up with stone so strong, my fair lady.

Stone so strong will last so long, last so long, last so long.
Stone so strong will last so long, my fair lady.

Los Pollitos Dicen

Words and Music
Tradtional
Arranged by
Hal Wright

Los po-lli-tos di-cen: "pí-o, pí-o, pí-o," cuan-do tie-nen ham-bre, cuan-do tie-nen frí-o.

Lullaby, Lullaby

Words and Music
Traditional
Arranged by
Hal Wright

Softly in the cradle lie, sleep, my darling, sleep.

Mammy Loves and Pappy Loves

Words and Music
Traditional
Arranged by
Hal Wright

Pap - py loves and Mam - my loves her lit - tle

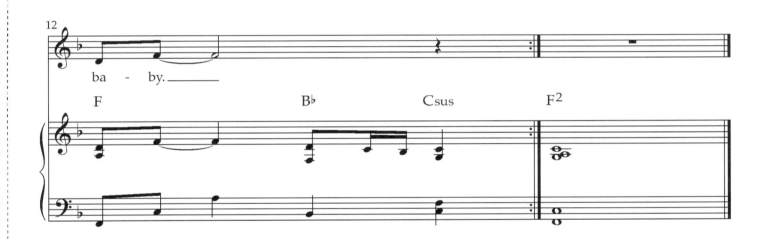

ba - by. ____

Mary Had a Little Lamb

Words and Music
Traditional
Arranged by
Hal Wright

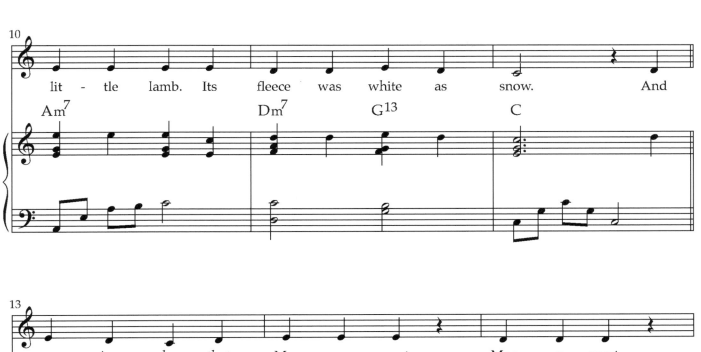

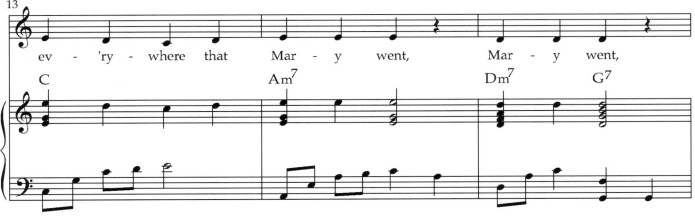

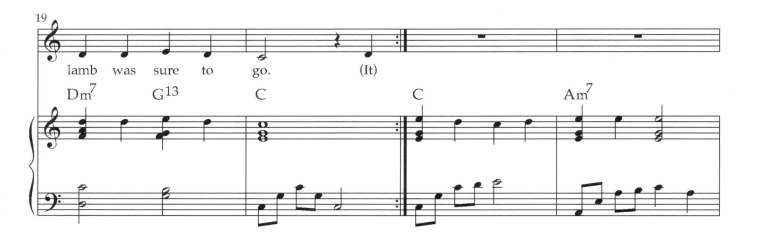

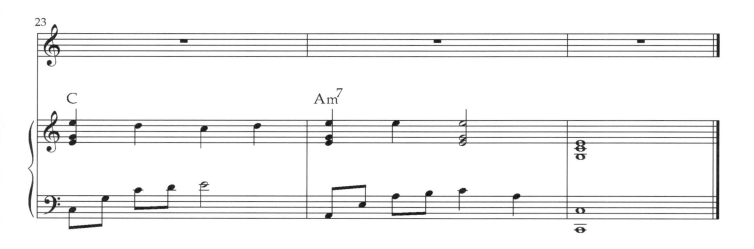

It followed her to school one day, school one day, school one day.
It followed her to school one day, which was against the rules.

It made the children laugh and play, laugh and play, laugh and play.
It made the children laugh and play to see a lamb at school.

And so the teacher turned it out, turned it out, turned it out.
And so the teacher turned it out, but still it lingered near

and waited patiently about, patiently about, patiently about,
and waited patiently about till Mary did appear.

"Why does the lamb love Mary so? Love Mary so? Love Mary so?"
"Why does the lamb love Mary so?" the eager children cry.

"Why, Mary loves the lamb, you know, lamb, you know, lamb, you know."
"Why, Mary loves the lamb, you know," the teacher did reply.

Mozart's Lullaby

Words and Music
Wolfgang Amadeus Mozart
Arranged by
Hal Wright

Now the Day Is Over

Words and Music
Traditional
Arranged by
Hal Wright

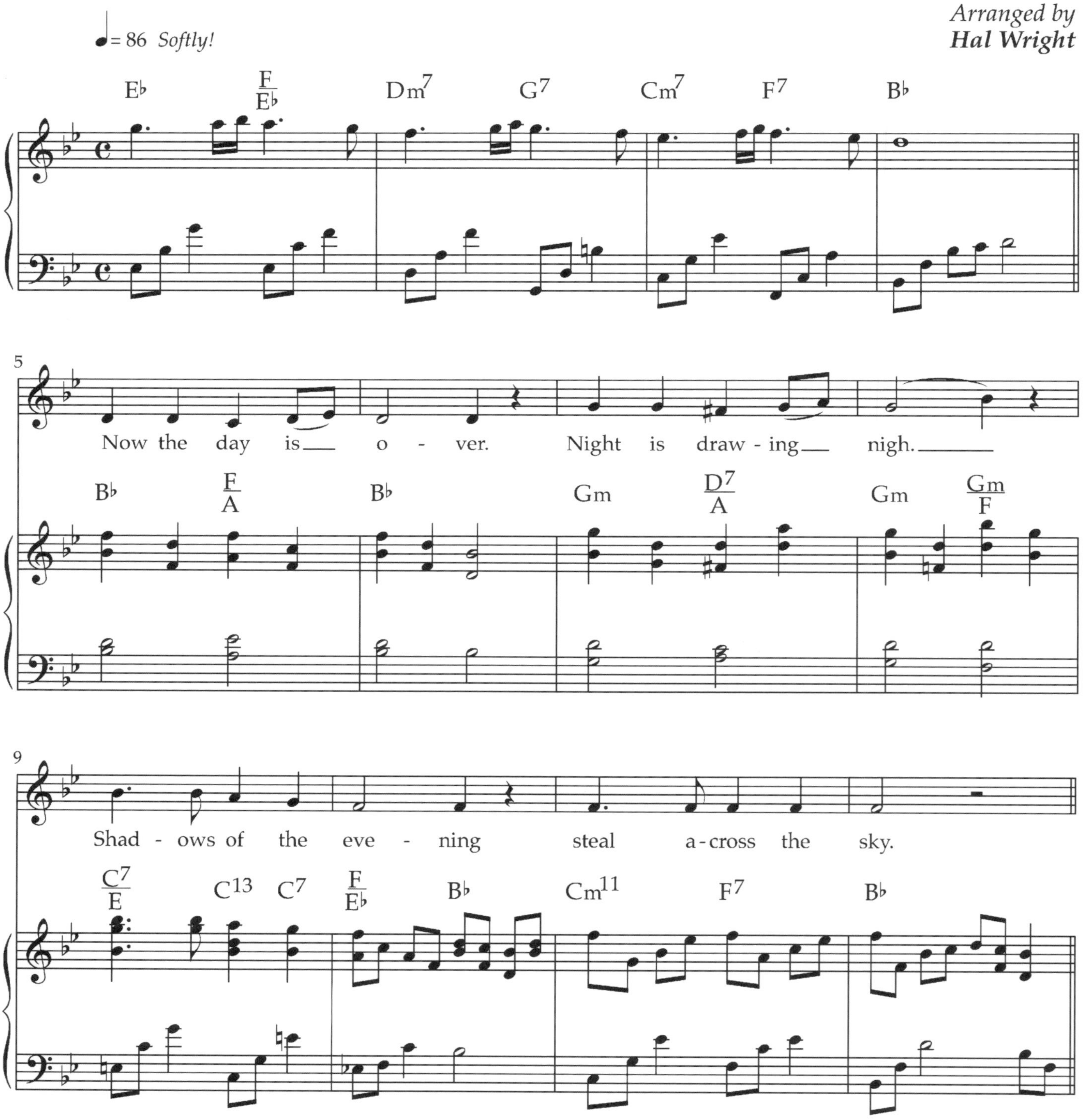

= 86 Softly!
E♭ F/E♭ Dm7 G7 Cm7 F7 B♭
5
Now the day is o - ver. Night is draw - ing nigh.
B♭ F/A B♭ Gm D7/A Gm Gm/F
9
Shad - ows of the eve - ning steal a-cross the sky.
C7/E C13 C7 F/E♭ B♭ Cm11 F7 B♭

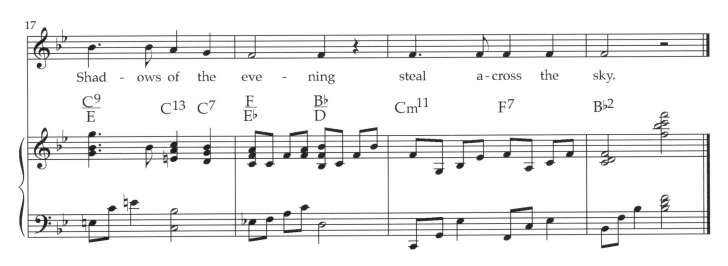

Oh Where, Oh Where
Has My Little Dog Gone?

Words and Music by
Septimus Winner
Arranged by
Hal Wright

Pussycat, Pussycat

Words and Music
Traditional
Arranged by
Hal Wright

fright - ened   a   lit - tle   mouse   un - der   her   chair.

Raisins and Almonds

Words and Music
Traditional
Arranged by
Hal Wright

Rock-a-Bye Baby

Words and Music
Traditional
Arranged by
Hal Wright

Rockin'

Words and Music
Traditional
Arranged by
Hal Wright

♩ = 96 *Sweetly!*

Lit - tle ba - by, sweet - ly___ sleep, do not___ weep. Sleep in___ com - fort.___ Slum - ber___ deep.

Sleep, Baby, Sleep

Words and Music
Traditional
Arranged by
Hal Wright

Sou Gan

Words and Music
Traditional
Arranged by
Hal Wright

Sleep, my ba - by, on my bo - som. Warm and coz - y, it will prove.

Round thee moth - er's arms are fold - ing. In her heart, a moth - er's love.

© 2006 Twin Sisters IP, LLC. All Rights Reserved.

Read, Sing, and Play Along! Lullaby Songs **299**

Swing Low, Sweet Chariot

Words and Music
Traditional
Arranged by
Hal Wright

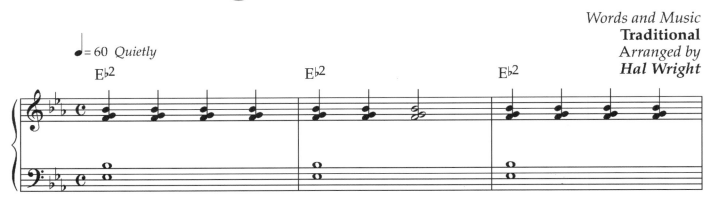

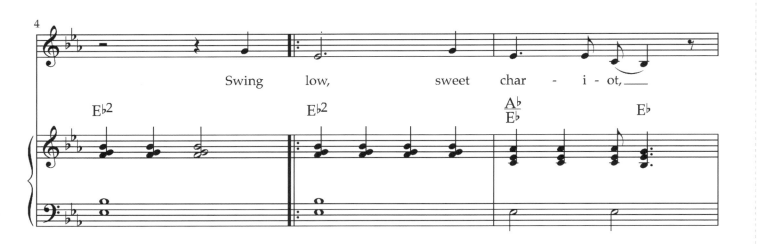

Swing low, sweet char - i - ot, ___

com-ing for to car-ry me home. Swing __ low, sweet

The Sandman Comes

Words and Music
Traditional
Arranged by
Hal Wright

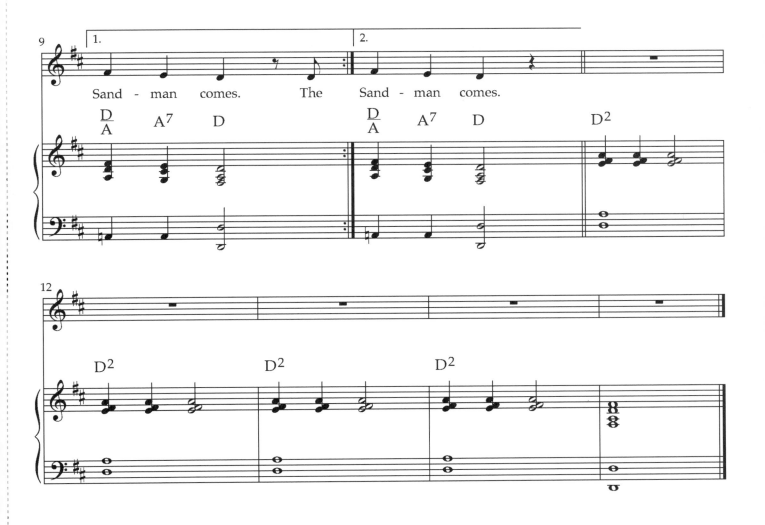

Sand - man comes. The Sand - man comes.

Three Blind Mice

Words and Music
Traditional
Arranged by
Hal Wright

three   blind   mice?

Three Little Kittens

Words and Music
Traditional
Arranged by
Hal Wright

sad - ly fear our mit - tens we have lost." _____ "What!
here, see here, our mit - tens we have found." _____ "What!
great - ly fear our mit - tens we have soiled." _____ "What!
here, look here, our mit - tens we have washed." _____ "What!

G   D⁷   G

Lost   your mit - tens? You naugh - ty kit - tens! Then
Found   your mit - tens? You dar - ling kit - tens! Then
Soiled your mit - tens? You naugh - ty kit - tens!" Then
Washed your mit - tens? You dar - ling kit - tens! But

Em   Em

Toora, Loora, Loora

Words and Music
Traditional
Arranged by
Hal Wright

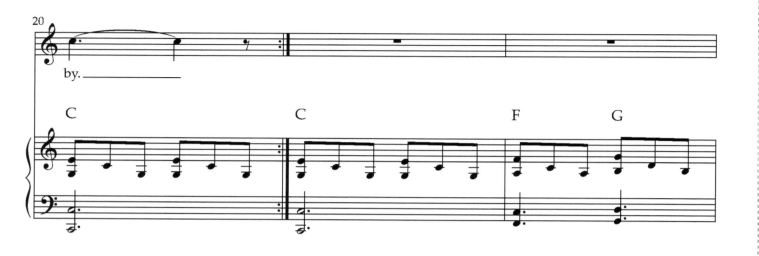

by. _____

Twinkle, Twinkle, Little Star

Words and Music
Traditional
Arranged by
Hal Wright

Bedtime Stories Log

	Date	Book Title	Author	Reading Buddy
1.				
2.				
3.				
4.				
5.				
6.				
7.				
8.				
9.				
10.				
11.				
12.				
13.				
14.				

Date	Book Title	Author	Reading Buddy
15.			
16.			
17.			
18.			
19.			
20.			
21.			
22.			
23.			
24.			
25.			
26.			
27.			
28.			
29.			
30.			